GHOST SHIP: The Confederate Raider *Alabama*

The Confederate warship ALABAMA is the most successful
commerce raider in modern history. During her two-year
career she destroyed more than sixty Union merchant
ships. GHOST SHIP is a fascinating account of this
famous ship. The author's style is most readable and
his description of the final battle between the ALABAMA
and the U.S.S. KEARSARGE is the most descriptive that I
have read. I highly recommend this book.

                    -- William N. Still, Jr.
                       Professor in History,
                       East Carolina University
                       Program in Maritime History
                       and Underwater Research

The C.S.S. *Alabama* destroying
a Union merchant ship.

GHOST SHIP

The Confederate
Raider
Alabama

Norman C. Delaney

Southfarm Press
Middletown, Connecticut

This Trade Paperback Edition
is published by
SOUTHFARM PRESS
A Division of Haan Graphic Publishing Services, Ltd.
P.O. Box 1296, 8 Yellow Orange Circle
Middletown, CT 06457

By arrangement with
Norman C. Delaney

ISBN: 0-913337-15-3
Library of Congress Catalog Card Number: 89-60317

First Printing: April, 1989
Printed in the United States of America

This work was previously published as part of
John McIntosh Kell of the Raider Alabama by Norman C. Delaney;
University, Alabama: The University of Alabama Press; 1973.

To Dad,
William L. Delaney,
With love and thanks

The C.S.S. *Alabama* and U.S.S. *Kearsarge* fight it out,
June 19, 1864.

Illustrations in this edition are courtesy of: Dover
Publications, Inc., pages 53, 55 (engraving by J. M. Butler);
Library of Congress (Brady-Handy Collection), page 18;
United States Navy, pages 2-3, 6-7, 8, 13, 20, 36, 45, 47, 52,
56, 60, 62, 66, 76, 78, 80, 82.

Cover art entitled "*Alabama* and *Kearsarge*" by Edouard
Manet (1832-1883). Courtesy of Philadelphia Museum of
Art, John G. Johnson Collection of Philadelphia.

Contents

President of the Confederate States of America.

TO ALL unto these Presents shall come, Send Greetings-

Know Ye, That we have granted, and by these Presents do grant, License and Authority to *Raphael Semmes* called the *Steamer Alabama*, Commander of the *Steamer Alabama*, of the Burden of Tons *1200* or thereabout, and mounting *Eight* Guns to fit out and set forth the said *Raphael Semmes* in a warlike Manner, and by and with the said

and the crew thereof, by Force of Arms, to attack, subdue, scuttle, and take all ships belonging to the United States of America or any vessel carrying Soldiers, Arms, Gunpowder, Ammunition, Provisions, or any other goods of a military nature to any of the Army of the United States or Ships of War employed against the Confederate States of America in a hostile manner. And to take by force if necessary any vessel, barge, or floating transporter belonging to said United States or persons loyal to the same, including Tackle, Apparel, Ladings, Cargoes, and Furniture on the High Seas or between high and low water mark, Rivers and Inlets excepted. (the Ships and Vessels belonging to Inhabitants of Bermuda, the Bahama Islands, and Great Britain and other persons with Intent to settle or serve the cause of the Confederate States of America you shall suffer to pass unmolested, the Commanders thereof permitting a peaceable Search and after giving satisfactory account of Ladings and Destination) And that said Ships or Vessels apprehended as aforesaid, and the Prize taken, to carry to a Port or Harbor within the Domaine of any Neutral State willing to admit the same or any port of the Confederate States, in Order that the Courts therein instituted to hear such claims may Judge in such cases at the Port or in the State where the same shall be impounded. The sufficient securities, bonds and sureties having been given by the owners that they nor any person in command of this vessel shall not exceed or transfer the Powers and Authorities contained in this commission. And We will and require all Officers whatsoever in the Service of the Confederate States to give assistance to the said in the Premises. This Commission shall remain active and in Force until this Government of the United Confederate States of America shall issue Orders to the contrary.

By order of the President of the

Confederate States of America

Port of _____

Given under my hand this *22nd* of *June* 186*2*

at *Richmond*

Jefferson Davis

President

Captain Raphael Semmes commission to command the C.S.S. Alabama was signed by Jefferson Davis on June 22, 1862.

Foreword

It has been one hundred and twenty-five years since the C.S.S. *Alabama* fought and lost her dramatic duel with the U.S.S. *Kearsarge*. Only recently, however — in 1984 — divers identified the *Alabama* in 180 feet of water, approximately 4 miles off the coast of France. It seems only a matter of time before cannon and other *Alabama* artifacts will be salvaged, preserved, and exhibited to the public. Because of their historic ties to the famous raider, three nations — the United States, Great Britain, and France — all have a strong interest in salvaging her.

From her beginning, the *Alabama* was truly international. Specially designed by Confederate naval agent James Dunwoody Bulloch as a swift greyhound of the seas, she was built in England by masters of the shipbuilders' craft. Her officers and crew included Englishmen, Southerners, and even men from New England.

Her dedicated captain — Raphael ("Old Beeswax") Semmes, C.S.N. — did much to help create the *Alabama* legend. She earned the titles "ghost ship" and "terror of the seas" by destroying millions of dollars worth of Northern commerce, and engaging and sinking the United States warship *Hatteras*. When she herself finally was sunk by the U.S.S. *Kearsarge*, thousands of spectators at Cherbourg witnessed the event. Her legend continues. The story of the "ghost ship" is timeless; it is one of courageous men at war.

Norman C. Delaney
Corpus Christi, Texas
January, 1989

1

C.S.S. *Sumter*

John McIntosh Kell was gratified by his new position. His orders to New Orleans had been personally approved by Commander Raphael Semmes, who had remembered the young midshipman of twelve years before. Semmes later wrote: "When it was decided, at Montgomery, that I was to have the *Sumter*, I at once thought of Kell, and, at my request, he was ordered to the ship." The ship in question, the *Havana* (a former mail steamer on the New Orleans to Havana line), was to be refitted and commissioned as the *Sumter*, the first of the Confederate commerce raiders. Semmes was anxious for the chance to cripple Northern resources through this means. Kell, as his "luff,"*could perform more valuable service for his country on the high seas than on the pitifully inadequate *Savannah*, his previous ship.

The *Sumter*, however, would not be ready for several weeks; then, she must be gotten past the blockade. Throughout May and into June they worked, until the ship could hardly be recognized as the former *Havana*.

As the *Sumter* stood downriver awaiting an opportunity to elude the U.S.S. *Brooklyn*, Kell made arrangements for his family's welfare. The Confederate Navy Agent was to provide his wife with an allotment of $100 per month for the next two years. Among the last tokens of love sent to Vineville

*"luff" was sailor jargon for first lieutenant aboard a vessel. The word is obsolete in today's navy.

11

was a package containing toys for the children and a recent daguerreotype for his wife. He wrote that the *Sumter* would have no announced cruising schedule as her movements were secret. With a "pleasant set of officers, a good crew, and a fine ship," he was optimistic about success.

On June 30 the *Sumter* made a hairbreadth escape to the open sea, after which her officers and crew drank a toast to their present and future success. That evening one of the *Sumter's* officers wrote in his journal:

> The Sumter has run the blockade at last! She is now bounding over the blue waters of the Gulf of Mexico; and if she does not soon slacken speed she will ere many days be in the Caribbean Sea. Everything was managed admirably.

Kell's wife learned of the escape of the *Sumter* through newspapers. It would be months before she would receive firsthand news from her husband, but meanwhile the picture taken of him at New Orleans would be some comfort. It showed a resolute, determined-looking man of erect bearing. However, the closely trimmed beard and shaven upper lip would not remain so; at the time he left New Orleans, Kell vowed that no razor or scissors would touch his face until he was once again with his family. After several months at sea, the most outstanding feature of Semmes' "luff" would be "a magnificent beard, inclining to red." Along with Kell's impressive height and bearing, the beard made him appear even more the dedicated, veteran sea dog. In contrast, Semmes' carefully waxed moustaches and imperial-style chin whiskers (earning him the nicknames "Old Beeswax," "Old Bim," and "Marshall Pomp" by his sailors) made him appear more of a scholar than a naval officer. Semmes, although a highly competent officer, possessed certain traits that had made him a controversial figure even before his present assignment. He was not one whom most men could get to know well, and he had long been known as a maverick and a loner. Semmes took his causes seriously, and he was now utterly devoted to serving the new Confederacy in the best way he could. Fortunately for both Semmes and Kell, they could work together effectively. Semmes had made an ideal choise of a "luff." However, this

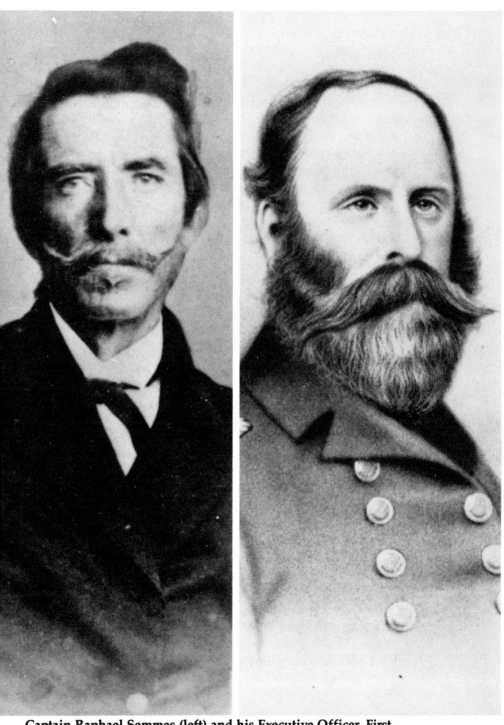

Captain Raphael Semmes (left) and his Executive Officer, First
Lieutenant John M. Kell (right).

was no partnership; Semmes was number *one* on his ship and expected the complete loyalty of his officers and men. In later years Kell admitted to his wife: "I could not remonstrate with Captain Semmes; he was my superior officer and fifteen years my senior."

After the war Kell would publicly reveal little of his relationship with Semmes, nor would he write of his commander except in the most complimentary terms. In Kell, Semmes had a man who met the most rigid requirements of his position. As naval authority Roe has observed: "The relations of the captain and the executive officer must be intimate and to a great degree confidential. There must be mutual confidence, or there will be mutual distrust." Dr. Francis L. Galt, the officer who was closest to both Semmes and Kell, bears this out: "[Kell's] cordial co-operation with his commander led to very pleasant intimate relations." Another glimpse of the relationship between the two is revealed in the recollections of a Confederate midshipman who served aboard C.S.S. *Georgia*:

> Captain Semmes was an austere and formal man, and with the exception of Dr. Galt, the surgeon, and Mr. Kell, his first lieutenant, he rarely held any intercourse with his officers except officially. He waxed the ends of his mustache (which the sailors called his "st'unsail booms") and he would pace the quarter-deck alone, twisting and retwisting those long ends.

As Semmes saw it, his position necessitated his being reserved and solitary most of the time. Thus his communications with his officers were usually restricted to affairs concerning the ship. It would be a mistake, though, to assume that Semmes was different from most other commanders in his official behavior. His officers and sailors apparently felt a great deal of respect for him, and Semmes was wise enough to know the pitfalls of overexposure or familiarity for one in high command. As Roe observed:

> There is a natural feeling among the crew of every ship, of aver-

sion to see the captain too frequently prowling about, as if seeking to find fault with someone. An instinctive feeling betrays itself, that the captain had better be in his cabin, or taking a quiet walk upon his quarter-deck.

However, Semmes was not always happy with this situation; he wrote, "I felt exceedingly its irksomeness, and was always glad of an opportunity to escape from it."

On the morning of January 18, 1862, a group of the British officers stationed at Gibraltar had accompanied Sir William J. Codington, Governor General of the Crown Colony, to the highest elevation of the Rock. There (at 1450 feet above sea level) they could clearly see a vessel aflame several miles away, off the Spanish coast. They could also see another vessel, soon identified as the *Sumter*. One of the Canadian officers—Lieutenant Brown Wallis of the 100th Regiment—years later recalled: "No one had any idea that the *terrible pirate* 'Sumter' was on our side of the Atlantic much less *in* the Mediterranean Sea."
At 7 p.m. the *Sumter* rounded Europa Point, entered the Bay of Gibraltar, and came to anchor off the "Old Mole." She had had one of her more successful days, having captured the bark *Neapolitan* (which was burned) and *Investigator* (which, because of her neutral cargo, was released on bond). During a six-month cruise of the Caribbean, off the coast of Brazil, and now near Spain, the *Sumter* had captured eighteen American merchantmen, and of these seven had been burned. Kell, who could take credit with Semmes for her successes, was full of praise for the little ship: "Frail and unseaworthy at best, her career was a marvel.... No ship of her size, her frailness, and her armament ever played such havoc on a powerful foe!"
One of the British observers on Gibraltar who visited the *Sumter* after her arrival could hardly believe that this was the dreaded "pirate" ship they had heard so much about:

I could scarcely believe that so poor a vessel could have escaped so many dangers. She is a screw-steamer, with three masts, a funnel strangely out of proportion to her size, and a tall, black hull, so high out of water that she gives you the idea of being insufficiently ballasted. Four 32-pounders peeped from her sides, and a large 8-inch pivot-gun was on her main-deck forward. . . . Her unsightly appearance arises from the alterations that have been made in her decks. In order to afford more accommodation, and to give more cover for the engines and guns, a light temporary flush-deck has been built over what was originally the only deck of the ship. This raises her an additional ten feet out of water, and at the same time dwarfs her masts and funnel. She is crank and leaky. Her engines are partially above the lower-deck, and, with the object of preserving them from the effects of gunshot, they are surrounded by a cylindrical casing of 6-inch wood covered with half-inch bars —a very poor protection against an 8-inch shot. Her officers and crew number ninety in all. The latter are a hardy set of fellows, ready for any work— men who would stick at nothing. They are of all nations—even the Irish brogue was among them. The commander, Captain Semmes, is a reserved, determined-looking man, whose left hand knows not what his right doeth.

A number of other Britishers, including Lieutenant Brown Wallis, soon rowed out to the famous "pirate" ship. The young Confederate officer on deck escorted the men to the wardroom, where wine and conversation were enjoyed. As Wallis sat near the partly opened hatchway, he was startled to hear the booming "clarion" voice of an officer in the process of dressing down a junior officer for having allowed the visitors aboard. When Wallis met the officer of the "clarion" voice, he was thoroughly impressed. As he later recalled, the lieutenant— Kell—was the "embodiment and realization" of his ideal of a naval officer. During the weeks that followed, Confederate and Canadian became friends, and the latter did all he could to help Kell enjoy his visits to the Rock, even arranging for him to participate in a fox hunt in the adjacent cork forests. On a clear day later that spring, Wallis and Kell, with Lieutenant Robert T. Chapman of the *Sumter*, rode on horseback along the upper ramparts of the Rock. At anchor far below them were ships of all nations, the most striking being the *Warrior*, 380 feet long, the first ironclad vessel in the British navy. She was anchored off the Mole, within half a dozen cable lengths of the *Sumter*, and the latter vessel—less than half her size—looked pitifully "diminutive by contrast." Greatly impressed, Chapman said: "Oh, if we only owned that one ship we could lay waste every seaport city in the Northern states." Kell replied humorously: "Chapman, you are an impetuous fire-eater, and as your senior officer I must inform you that we wouldn't do anything of the kind, because it would not be necessary; for, like Davy Crockett's coon, they would 'crawl down.' "

In port there was no letup in Kell's duties, and he had great difficulty keeping a tight rein on the crew. At every port a certain amount of drunkenness, misconduct, and desertion was anticipated, but now a sizeable number of sailors saw no reason to remain any longer on the *Sumter*. Several of the deserters asked the American consul for protection, including George A. Whipple, a seaman who had been with the ship since New Orleans. Whipple was no Confederate; a native of Massachusetts who happened to be in New Orleans when war broke out, he had shipped on the *Sumter* to avoid being drafted into the army. His true feelings had been revealed when, returning drunk from shore leave, he shouted curses at Captain Semmes and the Confederate flag. Whipple's punishment was extreme; Semmes had him put in irons and a straitjacket and later tied up by his thumbs. Now at Gibraltar, Whipple was able to desert, swearing vengeance against the man who had ordered his punishment. He sought out the American consul and signed a deposition that the *Sumter* had received coal in a neutral port, a fact vehemently denied by Semmes. Later, Whipple shipped aboard the *Kearsarge,* one of the Federal vessels which had arrived to prevent the *Sumter* from escaping to sea. During the next two years aboard the *Kearsarge,* he would dream of revenge.

On the night of March 8, after the *Kearsarge* came to anchor "within a stone's throw" of the *Sumter,* the stillness of the night was broken by exuberant strains of "Dixie," countered by "The Star Spangled Banner." Some of the crew of the

James M. Mason, Confederate diplomat. As Special Confederate Commissioner to England, Mason sent Captain Semmes a telegram on the C.S.S. *Sumter* that triggered the decision to abandon the *Sumter* as being unseaworthy.

Kearsarge actually spoke of swimming over to the *Sumter* during the night to sink her.

Earlier, Kell and other officers had made a thorough inspection of their ship. Their report was not encouraging. Boilers, a condenser, important machinery, and the upper works required a complete overhaul; some of the planking was badly worm-eaten. For more than two and a half months, Semmes and his officers remained with the *Sumter*, until on April 7 a telegram arrived from James M. Mason, Special Confederate Commissioner to England. That evening Semmes summoned the wardroom officers to his cabin and asked each his opinion on whether or not to give up the *Sumter*. The decision was unanimous that it would be impossible to get her into proper condition. That night an officer wrote in his journal:

> This news is received on all hands with great joy. We are heartily sick of the life of inactivity we have been leading for the past three months, though much regret will be felt at leaving the old ship which has carried us over so many miles of ocean and through so many perils.

Kell felt the same way: "As we passed out of the harbor of Gibraltar we cast a lingering look at the little vessel that had been our 'home on the rolling deep' during those last exciting months." Kell's orders were to make his way back to the Confederacy and report by letter to Secretary Mallory.

Kell was soon aboard the English passenger steamer bound for Nassau. With him was his Cousin John E. Ward, who had long since resigned his appointment as United States Minister to China and was returning to Georgia. Arriving at Nassau on June 8, they found that port bustling with activity. Captain Maffitt was preparing to launch the Confederate raider *Oreto (Florida)* on what would be a highly successful cruise.

Only days from home and family, Kell received news that could only have caused deep anguish: he and Semmes were to return immediately to England. A new ship was being fitted out, and he was again to be Semmes' executive officer. Unlike the *Sumter*, however, this was to be a new and "superior" vessel.

On July 13 Semmes and Kell left Nassau and arrived back in England three weeks later. Their months aboard the *Sumter* would prove invaluable experience for them on their new ship, C.S.S. *Alabama*.

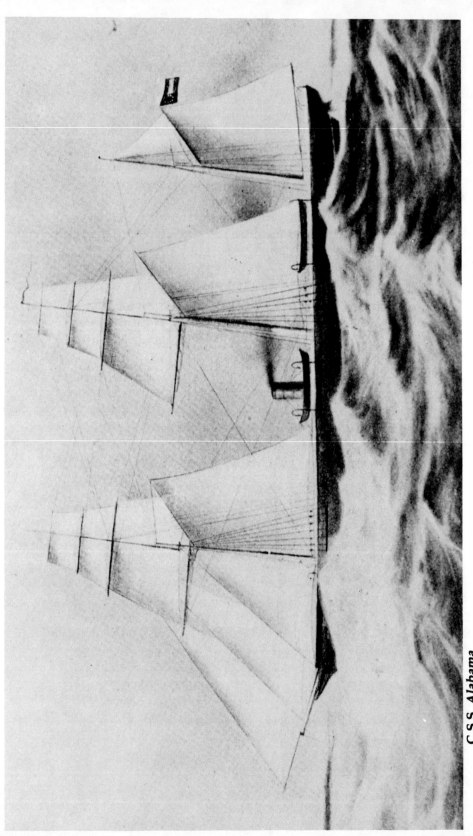

C.S.S. *Alabama*

2

C.S.S. *Alabama*

Arriving at Liverpool, the Confederate officers were surprised to find that "the bird had flown." The *290* (christened *Enrica* at her launching) had left port ten days earlier. However, Commander James Bulloch assured them that he had matters well in hand. Bulloch had ordered the *290* to sea to prevent her from being seized by British authorities. American agents in Britain had learned the purpose of the vessel recently launched at the Laird Shipyard and had demanded immediate seizure. Knowing he must act promptly, Bulloch had staged a mock trial run of the *Enrica* on July 29, complete with a party of guests to allay suspicion. That afternoon Bulloch explained to his guests that he wished to keep the ship out overnight, and they returned to Liverpool by tender. The escape of the *290* had been possible only because of luck and superb timing. Her temporary captain—Matthew J. Butcher, a confidant of Bulloch —had prepared the ship for sea, engaged a crew, and transacted the necessary business. Most of the crew knew the truth about the ship on which they had signed, but Bulloch had no intention of violating international law by enlisting a British crew for a Confederate vessel while within the United Kingdom. However, he had instructed his paymaster—Clarence R. Yonge—to "mix freely with the warrant and petty officers, show interest in their comfort and welfare, and endeavor to excite their interest in the approaching cruise." Yonge was directed to win friends for the cause of the Confed-

eracy by stressing its fight for "liberty." He was instructed
further:

> [Captain Semmes] will be a stranger to the ship and crew, and
> will be in a position of great responsibility and embarrassment.
> You have it in your power to smooth away some of his difficulties
> in advance.

Semmes, Kell, and Dr. Galt spent the next several days making preparations for their rendezvous with the *290*. Other
officers joined them, including Richard F. Armstrong of the
Sumter. Recognizing the competence of this officer, Semmes
had promoted him from midshipman to second lieutenant of
the *290*. Despite his youth (Armstrong had just turned twenty),
the young Georgian had more experience and proven ability
than the other available Southern officers except Kell. Of Armstrong, Kell would say, "he had all the requisities of a fine
and daring officer." Semmes' other senior officers (all young
men) included Joseph D. Wilson, a Floridian, as third
lieutenant; John Low, an Englishman, as fourth lieutenant;
and Arthur Sinclair, of an old naval family, as fifth lieutenant.
Then there were Becket K. Howell, a brother of Mrs. Jefferson
Davis, as marine officer (despite the fact that there would be
no marines aboard the *290*), and an Englishman, David H.
Llewellyn, as assistant surgeon under Dr. Galt. J. S. Bulloch,
brother of Commander Bulloch, served as acting master, while
Edward Anderson and Eugene Maffitt served as midshipmen.
Kell took a special interest in the careers of these young men.
The complement of officers was sufficient even before Semmes
left Liverpool.

On August 13 the Confederate officers, including Commander Bulloch, were aboard the steamship *Bahama*. Seven days
later they reached their point of rendezvous: Praya Bay at the
Island of Terceira in the Azores. They gazed eagerly at the
vessel for which the Confederates held such high hopes. For
Kell it was love at first sight. As he recalled many years later:
"I think she was the most beautiful ship that ever touched
the sea." Soon they were aboard her. After the fragile *Sumter*,

the *290* was close to luxury. She was built of the best available materials, copper-fastened, with condensing apparatus and a cooling tank to supply fresh water at sea. Under steam and sail (she was bark-rigged) the *290* was capable of speeds up to 13 knots. However, she would ordinarily be under sail—her hatches closed and chimney stack lowered—disguised as a merchant ship. No Confederate ensign would fly from her rigging until she had thus deceived her prey.

Bulloch already had a deep attachment to the ship to which he had "given so much care." He confessed: "Every aspiration of my heart is bound up in her." Originally, Bulloch was to have commanded the *290*, but the pressing need for his services as agent in England had prevented this. The Confederacy had to have ships built abroad for her infant navy.

The crew of the *290* was already busily engaged in transferring stores, coal, and heavy guns from the bark *Agrippina* (consort to the *290*) and would now transfer more guns, powder, and shell from the *Bahama*. The work continued over the next three days, after the vessels were moved outside Portuguese territorial waters to avoid any incident with the authorities. All went well, despite the difficulties created by the ocean swells.

Semmes was still left with the problem of enlisting a crew. He had been sizing up the sailors, including those who had arrived with him on the *Bahama*. By now few were ignorant of the identity and mission of the *290*. Shrewdly, a number of sailors refused to commit themselves. Semmes noted: "The sharp fellows, thinking I am dependent upon them for a crew, are holding back and trying to drive a hard bargain with me."

On August 24 the vessels headed for open sea; several miles off the harbor, Semmes made his move. Aboard the *Bahama* a starboard bow gun was fired, and on the *290* the English flag was hauled down and the Confederate ensign—a "splendid white flag" with cross and stars in the upper quarter—was raised. The band broke into "Dixie," followed by cheers from the officers and sailors on both vessels. The *290* was now the Confederate States Steamer *Alabama*. Semmes, admittedly "nervous about the success of this operation," had all hands piped aft to the quarter-deck of the *Bahama*. His secretary, Breedlove Smith, read Semmes' commission and orders from the Confederate government. Then Semmes addressed the men:

> Now, my lads, there is the ship; she is as fine a vessel as ever floated. There is a chance which seldom offers itself to a British seaman—that is, to make a little money. I am not going to put you alongside of a frigate at first, but after I have got you drilled a little, I will give you a nice little fight. There are only six ships that I am afraid of in the U.S. Navy. We are going to burn, sink, and destroy the commerce of the United States. Your prize-money will be divided proportionately, according to each man's rank, something similar to the English Navy.... There is Mr. Kell on the deck, and all who are desirous of going with me, let them go aft, and give Mr. Kell their names.

Semmes addressed those he saw holding back: "Any of you that thinks he cannot stand to his gun, I don't want."

The men who signed were motivated primarily by Semmes' promise of generous pay and prize money—in gold—good food, kind treatment, and grog served twice a day. Kell would admit: "A sailor is a sailor. He has few attachments, and as a general thing doesn't care what flag he is under." Semmes had been obliged to accept the men's terms. His seamen were promised a monthly L 4 10s., petty officers L 5 and L 6, and firemen L 7. But Semmes was glad to get the men on even these generous terms: "I was afraid a large bounty in addition would be demanded of me." With a crew of eighty-two sailors, he needed forty more men to make up a full complement. That evening was spent in preparing allotments for the wives of some of the men and paying two months advance wages. Except for occasional small allowances, the men would not receive the rest of their pay until the end of the cruise. Prize money was to be paid after the war had ended. One of the English sailors who signed on that day penned in his journal: "I became a naval sailor in this fine ship. I shall be happy and perhaps become rich." The man was favorably impressed with his new captain: "He is always kind and polite to everyone and he speaks like a Devon man. I think that he is a fine and good man."

Late at night Commander Bulloch, accompanied by Captain Butcher and the sailors who refused to sign on the *Alabama*, steamed away on the *Bahama* back to Liverpool. Semmes lost no time in setting his own course for open sea. The next morning the *Alabama* rolled and tumbled in the North Atlantic as Kell began the job of getting things organized. Semmes, retiring below "to quiet worn nerves," knew that his "luff" had no easy job ahead. He noted in his journal: "The first lieutenant is trying to bring order out of chaos, in getting his crew into shape." It would take a week to put the ship in order. The most urgent work was getting the eight guns (six 32-pounders and two pivot guns—an 8-inch solid shot and a 100-pound Blakely rifled gun) ready for firing and the men assigned to battle stations. Kell, the office responsible for disciplining and drilling the crew, found them to be a "mixture." Thirty or so were "very fine, adventurous seamen," but the remaining fifty, from the slums of Liverpool, "looked as if they would need some man-of-war discipline to make anything of them." Semmes was quite frank in his evaluation: "One has all sorts of characters to deal with in a ship's crew, and a vigorous arm is necessary. The boys . . . are most incorrigible young rascals." It would take three months before Semmes considered his crew to be in "fair fighting trim." He took satisfaction in maintaining the discipline he considered appropriate for a ship-of-war:

My code was like that of the Medes and Persians—it was never relaxed. The moment a man offended, he was seized and confined in irons, and, if the offense was a grave one, a court-martial was sitting on his case in less than twenty-four hours. The willing and obedient were treated with humanity and kindness; the turbulent were jerked down, with a strong hand, and made submissive to discipline. I was as rigid with the officers as with the crew, though, of course, in a different way. . . . My crew were never so happy as when they had plenty to do, and but little to think about. Indeed, as to the thinking, I allowed them to do very little of that.

In spite of this, the depositions of sea captains and mates from vessels captured by the *Alabama* indicate something of the difficulties being faced by Semmes and his officers. One observed: "The officers are Southerners, and with the exception of the captain and first lieutenant seem ignorant of their sea duties. The discipline on board was not very good, though the men seemed to be good seamen. They were over an hour setting the two top-gallant sails." And another: "I observed that there was no discipline on board the steamer excepting when Capt. Semmes or Lieut. Kell was on deck." Semmes himself—in entries in his journal—gives ample evidence of dissatisfaction on the part of the crew. As he believed, many of his sailors "thought they were shipping in a sort of privateer, where they would have a jolly good time and plenty of license." He observed:

> Constant cruising, vigilance against being surprised by the enemy, salt provisions, and a deprivation of the pleasures of port . . . are probably what most of them did not expect. A tight rein and plenty of work will cure the evil.

The sailors were not the only ones who needed disciplining. Chief Engineer Miles J. Freeman, who had served in the same capacity aboard the *Sumter*, was suspended for disobeying orders and using "improper language" to Kell. As Semmes saw the incident: "Engineers in general seem to think that they have a sort of separate command, and that they are, to some extent, independent of the first lieutenant." It was not long, however, before Freeman was reinstated as chief engineer.

The *Alabama* had been at sea ten days when—on September 5th—the whaling ship *Ocmulgee* was sighted. She was to be the first of sixty-five prizes of the Confederate raider during the twenty-two months of her cruise. Semmes' orders were to destroy the commerce of the North, but to avoid engagements with the enemy's vessels of war. In the case of the *Ocmulgee*, capture was easy, as her crew were at work on a whale lashed alongside the ship. The officers were allowed to bring off a trunk of clothes each and the sailors a bag apiece. Stores from the prize were brought aboard the *Alabama*, and the next morning she was burned. Aboard the *Alabama* the officers of the *Ocmulgee* were put in irons in retaliation for the treatment of Paymaster Myers of the *Sumter*. The use of irons would continue with the prisoners (officers and sailors alike) taken from the first several captures, but it ended after Semmes felt that he had made his point. Kell described the usual method of taking a prize:

> As soon as we sighted a ship we would hail her. If she didn't stop we would fire a blank cartridge across her bow. If she still refused to respond we would send a shot in front of her, and that would bring her to. Our long-range guns were of invaluable service in this business. When we hailed a ship we generally had the U.S. flag flying and kept it up until we were alongside. Then we would lower a boat and send an officer on board; but just before he boarded her the U.S. flag would come down and up would go the Confederate flag. Our officer would go to the captain of the ship we had caught, demand his papers, order him into the boat and bring him on board. Admiral Semmes always remained in his cabin when a capture was made and the captains of our prizes were taken before him there. He examined their papers and questioned them closely. If the ship was found to belong to a citizen of a neutral country, a fact which the captain's papers would always reveal, she was at once released. When we discovered that we had the property of a citizen of the United States we took her officers, crew and passengers (if she had any) on board. We then went through her cargo and appropriated what we needed—for . . . we lived almost entirely on our prizes. When we had all we wanted, we set fire to the captured ship and sailed away to look for another.

Either Kell or Armstrong would estimate the value of the prize, because in cases of an American-owned vessel carrying neutral-owned cargo, the vessel would be released on bond. This meant that the value of the vessel was to be paid to the Confederate government by her owners at the conclusion of hostilities. When a ship was so released, she was obliged to relieve Semmes of all his prisoners.

Kell, who supervised the distribution of every prize, made it a hard and fast rule that no boat's crew could board the

vessel until after all the liquor found aboard was thrown overboard or placed in a safe place. This policy caused a great
deal of dissatisfaction among those sailors looking for oppor-
tunities to loot. For these men, the daily ration of grog—served
morning and noon by an officer aboard the *Alabama*—
was inadequate.   In spite of all the precautions taken, however, liquor was frequently smuggled aboard the *Alabama* from
the prizes. Semmes and Kell were continually troubled by the
results of these violations of discipline. Even their best sailors,
they found, could not be trusted with whisky.

After supplies had been transferred to the *Alabama*—along
with charts and chronometers—the boarding officer would
direct the men in breaking up furniture or gathering mattresses.
Lard or other inflammable liquid would be poured on this,
and a fire set. Watching a burning ship had a certain exhilarat-
ing effect upon Kell. He wrote:

> To watch the leaping flames on a burning ship gives an indescrib-
> able mental excitement that did not decrease with the frequency
> of the light, but it was always a relief to know the ships were
> tenantless as they disappeared in lonely grandeur, specks of
> vanishing light in the "cradle of the deep."

Within five weeks after the burning of the *Ocmulgee*, the
Confederates had consigned a dozen more vessels, mostly
whalers, to the flames, and this was only the beginning.
However, one vessel, the *Tonawanda*—carrying a cargo of grain
—was spared because of the women and children aboard for
whom the *Alabama* lacked proper accommodations. The ship
was used as "bait" to lure another ship for an easy capture
and to carry off the prisoners taken since leaving the Azores.
Aboard another ship—the brigantine *Dunkirk*—was a deserter
from the *Sumter*, seaman George Forrest. Semmes ordered a
court-martial to decide Forrest's punishment, and it was
decided that he should serve without pay on the *Alabama* for
the remainder of the cruise. However, he would be eligible
to share in prize money.

Far more important than the deserter Forrest were the new

volunteers coming from captured vessels. Semmes soon had thirty additional sailors and was only ten short of his full complement of one hundred and twenty. By the end of the cruise he would have an assortment of sailors representing most of the seafaring nations. Kell admitted to his own favorite class of seamen: "The thoroughbred downeaster is the best seaman that sails the ocean. He is handy and trusty and has little dread of storms or shells. Next to him, and in special directions superior to him, is the British tar."

After cruising the vicinity of the Azores for as long as he felt it wise, the *Alabama* was headed toward Newfoundland, while Semmes planned a move that—if successful—might prove a turning point in the war. Because his plan had to be scrapped, Semmes never mentioned it in his writings. However, Kell did. The plan called for the *Alabama* to be brought into New York City's outer harbor at night. There, the merchant ships were to be boarded and their crews transferred to the lightship, after which the ships were to be set afire. The *Alabama* would make her escape before dawn.

A hundred miles off George's Bank—on October 16—the *Alabama* ran into a cyclone, one of the worst ever experienced by Kell. The hatches were battened down and life lines passed along the decks to keep the men from being washed overboard. As the barometer continued to fall, the sea became "one sheet of foam and spray from the violence of the wind." The ship rolled and plunged, head and stern, taking tons of water on her decks. The winds tore away the main brace, the main yard snapped in two, and the maintopsail was torn into shreds. Working under great difficulty, the men succeeded in securing the main yard and lowering the spars to the deck. Suddenly all was calm. Anticipating what would happen next, Semmes said to his "luff": "Mr. Kell, in a few minutes we will get the wind with renewed violence in the opposite direction." Kell gave the necessary orders to the men, and the yards were braced and storm staysail secured. Minutes later, the storm came with even greater violence than before.   As Kell recalled of those terrible four hours: "It would be impossible to convey an adequate idea of the fury of the terrible typhoon."   That night, a sailor noted in his journal: "Only the skill of our Captain and Mr. Low, the Fourth Lieutenant, saved us from a watery grave."

Although within two hundred and fifty miles of New York City, Semmes decided to give up his plan of attack and attend to repairs. He also had to rendezvous with his coal ship, the *Agrippina*. As the *Alabama* sailed for Martinique in the Carribbean, she added six more vessels to her growing list of captures. From one of these—the *T.B. Wales*—the Confederates secured a main yard to replace their loss. With it in place they were "complete again in . . . sailing capacity." The capture of this ship brought an unexpected but not unpleasant surprise for the Confederates. As passengers were the U.S. Consul to Mauritius, his wife, and three young daughters: The latter soon became "very much at home" aboard the *Alabama*—where the best wardroom cabins were put at the disposal of the family. Kell would later write: "I feel sure they never denounced us as pirates."

Arriving at Fort de France on November 18, the Confederates found the *Agrippina* at anchor. Kell was sent to call on the French Admiral to report the arrival of the *Alabama*. He was "received . . . pleasantly" and given a warning. Captain Robert McQueen of the *Agrippina* had—under the influence of whisky—indiscreetly made known the identity of the vessel for which he was waiting. The Admiral advised that the *Alabama* be brought under the guns of the fort for protection before any American warships arrived. When Semmes learned of this, he ordered McQueen to proceed immediately to Blanquilla Island off the coast of Venezuela. He could not risk remaining at Martinique for his coaling.

Throughout the afternoon native "bumboats" brought their wares—fruits, tobacco, and pipes—to the *Alabama*. Not all the articles being brought on board were so innocent. Seaman George Forrest managed to get rum on board the ship and distributed to the roughest element in the crew. Forrest had had enough of the *Alabama* and was determined to take advantage of the opportunity to incite mutiny while in port. Late in the afternoon, after visitors had left the ship, Kell heard an uproar on the forecastle. Going forward to investigate, he was greeted by the curses and threats of at least a score of men. A belaying pin missed its mark as Kell stood his ground. He ordered those men who appeared to be sober to seize their drunken comrades, but not a hand was raised. When Semmes appeared, he saw a surly, defiant crowd of drunken sailors gathered together near the foremast. Most of the other sailors seemed hesitant. Semmes, realizing that the men had only sheath-knives and belaying pins, while his officers were well armed, turned to his "luff" and said: "Mr. Kell, give the order to beat to quarters." As drum and fife were heard, the men automatically fell in at their stations. Semmes and Kell then passed along the men as they stood at the guns. Semmes eyed each man, and whenever he observed one drunk, he ordered him seized by his comrades at station. Twenty sailors were taken and put in irons, and Semmes ordered them to the gangway, where buckets of sea water were to be dashed over them by the most rugged of the quartermasters. At first, the men laughed and swore: "Come on with your water; we're not afraid of it!" However, as bucket after bucket was emptied over them, they began to gasp and choke. Soon they were begging for mercy. An occasional snicker could be heard from the sober men still at their stations during the two-hour-long treatment. When Semmes thought the men had had enough, he gave the order to "beat the retreat." The irons were removed and the mutineers allowed to go below to their hammocks. Only Forrest, the ringleader, would be punished further. Semmes ordered him "spread eagled" in the rigging for stretches of four hours at a time. A court-martial would decide his ultimate fate. According to Semmes, the incident at Fort de France was the only case of mutinous conduct aboard the *Alabama*. As the ship left the French island the morning following the disturbance, one of the crew wrote in his journal: "Some of our fellows are very down-hearted. They say that the rats have all left our good ship and that we will soon be dead men." This time, however, the *Alabama* had gotten away in time. The U.S.S. *San Jacinto,* steaming outside the maritime limit in expectation of waylaying the *Alabama*, was successfully evaded in a night escape.

On November 26, at the barren island of Blanquilla, the

sentence of the court-martial was executed. Forrest was to be discharged in disgrace, having forfeited the right to any prize money. He was landed on the island with only the clothes he wore. The man was no loss to the *Alabama*. Years later Kell recalled Forrest as "a short, thickset fellow with dingy yellowish hair. . . . He was positively ugly and one of the most vicious fellows I ever knew."

The crew was allowed liberty on the island and issued rifles for hunting and sport. There was nothing else to do, as Blanquilla was inhabited only by four Spaniards who raised goats and jackasses. Midshipman E. Maffit Anderson, in charge of the liberty party, allowed the sailors to disregard Semmes' implicit orders. In a private letter, Anderson wrote of the men:

> They forgot themselves, and commenced killing goats, jackasses and everything else that they could come across. We all thought that it was very good fun, but it was good for all hands that Captain Semmes knew nothing of it.

After coaling at Blanquilla, Semmes set his course for the eastern end of Cuba. He was anxious to capture a New York-bound steamer carrying California gold for the United States Mint. On December 7 they captured the steamer *Ariel*, headed for Aspinwall on the Isthmus of Panama. Although she carried no gold, her safe contained $8,000 in U.S. Treasury notes and $1,500 in silver. Aboard were one hundred and forty marines, seven officers, and five hundred passengers, in addition to the regular crew. The passengers included a large number of terrified women and children. Among the naval officers was Commander Lewis C. Sartori, whom Kell remembered from the Pensacola Navy Yard. No word was exchanged between the two men who now found themselves on opposite sides of civil war.

Semmes had a special reason for wanting the *Ariel* burned: she was owned by Commodore Cornelius Vanderbilt, a bitter enemy of the Southern Confederacy. With Lieutenant Low in charge of the *Ariel*, she was escorted to Kingston, Jamaica. However, before he reached that port Semmes received a report of a fever epidemic there. The *Ariel* was then released on ransom bond. The Confederates took some little consolation in the loss of their prize. Commander Sartori had assured Low that he would correct "the erroneous rumors in circulation about the *Alabama*." As Sartori admitted, everyone aboard the *Ariel* had received "the most courteous treatment." Kell hoped that Sartori's word would help discredit the tales of "lawless piracy" circulating in the Northern press; on reflection, Kell decided that it did not really matter so long as the Southern cause was being strengthened by their efforts.

Semmes set his course for the desolate Las Arcas Islands, off Yucatan. Here during the last days of 1862, he put his ship in order: calking, painting, tarring, and taking on more coal. Since the small islands were devoid of all life except birds and sea turtles, the men were deprived of the "pleasures of port." They had to satisfy themselves with killing a few turtles and raiding the nests for eggs. Semmes felt that his discipline had finally brought results:

It has taken me three or four months to accomplish this, but when it is considered that my little kingdom consisted of 110 of the most reckless sailors from the groggeries and brothels of Liverpool, that is not much.

3

The Trials of War

It was four months since Semmes had taken command of the *Alabama*, and he believed he now had the "well disciplined ship of war" necessary for a bold strike at the enemy. Documents and newspapers taken from the *Ariel* had revealed that the Federals were preparing to launch an expedition of thirty thousand men under General Nathaniel P. Banks for an invasion of Texas. About a hundred vessels were to arrive off Galveston—already in Federal hands—about January 10 and land the troops. Semmes intended a surprise night attack, blasting away at the vessels of the fleet while running at full steam before making his escape. Nearing Galveston on the morning of January 11, a confident Semmes noted in his journal: "My crew are a fine looking body of men, have been well drilled, and are not adverse, I think, to a trial of skill and force with the enemy."

As the *Alabama* approached Galveston, the lookout was not alert, and they appeared in plain view of several vessels anchored off the bar. Observing that a gunboat was firing on the city, Semmes exclaimed: "Well, they would not be firing on their own people. Galveston is recaptured and Banks' great expedition a failure!" Shortly, one of the vessels was seen to be getting up steam. The *Alabama* stood under topsails while the stranger approached stern on. Semmes intended to draw her away from the rest of the fleet, knowing that distance and darkness would be his best allies in the event of a fight. It was already 4 p.m.

The approaching vessel was—unknown to the Confederates—the U.S.S. *Hatteras,* commanded by Homer C. Blake. The *Hatteras* was an iron side-wheel steamer (a former river excursion boat) with her engines exposed and unprotected. A Confederate naval authority later made the observation: "There is no doubt that the *Alabama* was the superior ship, and barring an accident . . . she ought to have won." Commander Blake was not naively sailing into Semmes' trap. After having signalled "Suspicious Sail," he had been ordered by the flagship *Brooklyn* to investigate. In his report, Blake admitted that, "from the general character of the vessel and her maneuvering," he expected to encounter "the rebel steamer *Alabama.*" Blake planned to close with the raider, since his guns were most effective at close range. At a distance of about 100 yards, he hailed: "What steamer is that?" The answer came back: "Her Britannic Majesty's Ship *Petrel.* Who are You?" Blake answered: "United States Ship - - - -" The name was lost in the wind. Finally Blake called out: "If you please, I will send a boat on board of you." During the exchange, both vessels had been maneuvering for better combat positions. They were twenty miles from the Federal fleet, and, at 6:30 p.m., it was dark. A boat from the *Hatteras* shoved off toward the *Alabama.*

To Semmes' question "Are you ready for action?" Kell replied, "The men are only waiting for the word." All were at their stations on the starboard battery; guns were set and loaded with 5-second shell. Semmes instructed Kell: "Don't strike them in disguise; tell them who we are, and give the broadside at the name." Raising his trumpet, Kell sang out: "This is the Confederate States Steamer *Alabama!*—Fire!" Flashes of flame spat out, and the Confederates' broadside struck iron. As she was struck repeatedly, the side of the Federal steamer lit up, showing long rents. The wind was now blowing in the direction of Galveston and the Union fleet. With no moon to guide them, the men had to judge the distance for sighting by the flash of enemy guns. Blake steamed directly for the *Alabama,* hoping to board her, but (he later complained) his speed was diminished by "foulness of bottom." The range

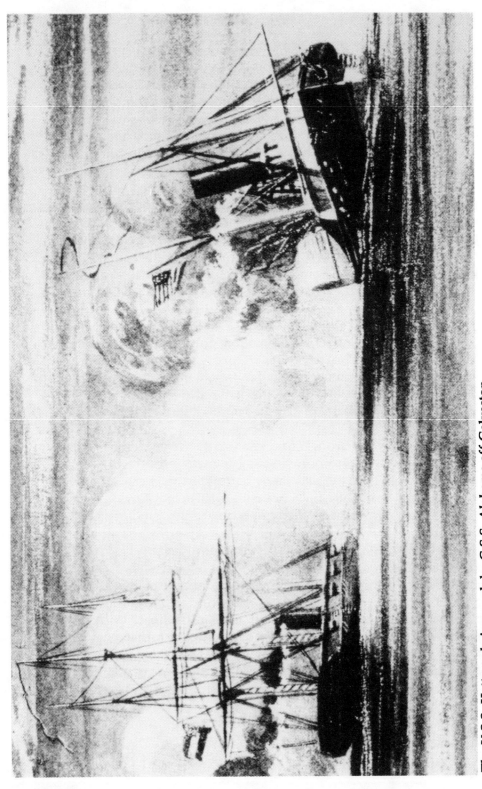

The U.S.S. *Hatteras* being sunk by C.S.S. *Alabama* off Galveston, Texas on January 11, 1863.

between the vessels was so close that musket and pistol shots were exchanged. The action became a running fight in parallel lines, with the vessels nearing then separating from each other. Semmes stood on the horse-block above the rail of his ship, observing the action as best he could. Unable to suppress his excitement, he called out to his gunners: "Give it to the rascals! Aim low, men! Don't be all night sinking that fellow!" The men were also caught up in the excitement as they sighted their guns. Whenever a shell struck home, a boatswain's mate exclaimed: "That's from 'the scum of England'!" "That's a British pill for you to swallow!" Shells entering the hold of the *Hatteras* were setting fires and causing explosions. One entered the cylinder and—with his engine room filling with steam—Blake could no longer maneuver his ship. The *Hatteras* was sinking rapidly. Blake ordered his magazine flooded to prevent the ship from blowing up and a lee gun to be fired in surrender. Only thirteen minutes had elapsed since the beginning of the action, during which the *Alabama* had fired eight broadsides. From his position on the horse block, Semmes called out: "Mr. Kell, the enemy have fired a gun to leeward; cease firing." As the order was given, over a hundred voices were raised in cheers. The raider steamed closer to the *Hatteras*, and Kell inquired whether they had surrendered. Hearing answering cries for assistance, Kell gave the order, "All hands out boats to save life!"

Within an hour, the Federal officers and sailors—a total of one hundred and twenty-six—were picked up and taken to the *Alabama*. When Commander Blake came on deck and delivered up his sword, Semmes finally learned the name of the ship he had sunk. Smacking his lips with pleasure, he gave up his stateroom to Blake, while the other officers were accommodated according to rank and the crew placed on the berth deck. The latter were placed in single irons. After rewarding his own crew with grog, Semmes made haste to get clear of possible pursuers; with her lights extinguished, the *Alabama* was soon far from the coast. The raider had not been seriously damaged, although one shell had narrowly missed the middle starboard gun crew. A second shell had gone through the

Alabama's side, under the main chains, and lodged in the opposite timbers, while another had ripped into and through the funnel. But Semmes and his men considered themselves fortunate to have come out of the contest so well. In a longer engagement the Blakely gun would certainly have caused difficulty, for—as Kell later stated—"It became easily heated, from deficiency in metal, and the powder charge would have to be reduced on account of the recoil."

The morning after the fight, while Kell was on deck supervising repairs, Commander Blake appeared. He recognized Kell and saluted him: "How do you do, Mr. Kell? Fortune favors the brave, sir." Kell thanked him and added, "We take advantage of all fortune's favors."

Nine days after her victory, the *Alabama* arrived at Kingston, Jamaica, to land the prisoners, take on coal, and make additional repairs. Soon after their arrival, Semmes gladly accepted the opportunity for a few days respite in the hills, leaving Kell in charge of the ship. As Semmes would one day write:

> Kell was of wonderful assistance to me, in this respect. I always left the ship in his hands, with the utmost confidence, and my confidence was never misplaced. He was ... an excellent disciplinarian, and being, besides, a thorough master of his profession, I had in him all that I could desire.

After three days of rest and seclusion, Semmes learned that the *Alabama* was ready for sea. However, all was not well; Paymaster Clarence Yonge had been "disgracing himself," and the liberty men had not returned to the ship. Yonge had gone ashore with L 400, supposedly to settle accounts, but had, instead, become thoroughly intoxicated. Learning of this, Kell had him carried aboard the ship under arrest. When Semmes returned he lost no time in ordering Yonge to pack up and leave the ship at once. Yonge was the only one of his officers whom Semmes was forced to discharge. The case was especially galling to Kell, who had recommended his own ardently Confederate brother-in-law, John Hutton, as paymaster. There still remained the problem of getting the liberty men back on board.

Kell would admit: "Carried away with victory, many of [the men] got gloriously drunk, and gave me a good deal of trouble to get them back and properly sobered."   Only with the aid of the local police were most of the missing sailors returned. Writing in his journal, Semmes was bitter as he observed: "It will take me at least a week to get the rum out of them, and to try the more vicious by court-martial."   On January 25 the *Alabama* proceeded to sea and headed toward the coast of South America.

Kell had time for occasional diversions. Lieutenant Sinclair would later describe Kell and Dr. Galt playing checkers and the "luff" entertaining the wardroom officers with stories of the old navy.   Kell's beard had become somewhat of a vanity by this time. Not only did it make Kell look older, but it tended to accentuate his important position aboard the ship. With it, he was easily mistaken for a British sea captain. Kell's beard had a devoted admirer in Bartelli, Semmes' steward. Bartelli "took pride and pleasure in brushing and platting [the] luxurious beard."   Kell himself wrote of evenings spent on the bridge, watching the light of burning ships, while he reflected on "man in his sinful nature warring with his brother man." During these moments, the officers would "seek the refreshing influences of past social enjoyments" by talking of "home and absent friends."   There were rare moments, too, when Semmes would join his officers in relaxed smoking and talking. A favorite topic of conversation was the South and the progress of the war. News of Confederate victories on land and sea never failed to lift the men's morale, while news of defeats was received with gloom. However, since most of what was read was found in Northern newspapers from captured prizes, they found reason to be skeptical of news that indicated Southern failures and defeats. References to the *Alabama* as an "infamous pirate" were infuriating; yet these gave satisfying evidence of how badly Northern commerce was being hurt. Semmes had a special admiration for a fellow "pirate"—John Maffitt—whose midshipman son was one of his own young officers. Kell would one day tell Maffitt of the "great admiration" Semmes felt toward him: "I can picture now his smile—he never laughed—which lit up every feature when narrating your deeds, especially your entrance and exit from Mobile Bay in the *Florida*."

One of Kell's social functions was presiding over the wardroom mess, where, because of Semmes' personal disdain for liquor, nothing stronger than claret was ever served, despite the fact that Semmes ate alone in his own cabin. Nor would Semmes allow card playing among his officers. It is doubtful whether Kell himself ever unbent with the officers (aside from Dr. Galt), who were so much younger than he. But as an observer, he naturally would have enjoyed the singing, musicmaking, dancing, and improvised plays of the sailors during the evening hours. At these times, "the discipline of the ship was wont to be purposely relaxed," and roars of laughter would resound from the forecastle. The entertainment invariably concluded with a rousing chorus of "Dixie," and a hundred or more voices were raised in "an uproar of enthusiasm."   At 8 p.m. all merriment came to an end as the night watches were set.

The man who knew Kell better than any other officer during the *Sumter* and *Alabama* cruises was Dr. Francis Galt. Years after the war, Galt recalled those years and his friend. According to Galt, Kell's "steadiness of temper" had been under the "firmest control." Concerning Kell's competence as an officer, he wrote: "The modesty of his nature . . . was guarded by an undeviating adherence to a line of action in his duties which made it very easy for those associated with him to know exactly what was to be expected of him." Galt added:

He had a very keen sense of injustice, and was always ready to remedy any act which showed a want of this elementary trait of human nature. Intent always in carrying out the details of his duties, perfectly content to see that his ship was the most important thing to attend to, and the natural curiosity of men to visit foreign places, to look at, or engage in any social functions had no power to prevent his first seeing that his duties as an officer were the first work in hand.

There was at least one other officer who felt differently. He

was Second Lieutenant Armstrong, a competent officer whose
capabilities were recognized by both Semmes and Kell. Armstrong was too good an officer to let the first lieutenant know
his personal feelings toward him or let them interfere with
his duties. It was only many years after the war that he confessed: "How I used to hate him. He used to make us youngsters
stand around, and after we were made lieutenants we thought
ourselves as important as he." Following the war, a more
mature Armstrong came to appreciate the qualities of his former
superior officer. He would say: "Captain Semmes may well
give him the credit of the discipline and much of the success
of the ship. It was duty, first, last, and always, with our first
officer, and no boyish nonsense either, except in our frolics
ashore on off duty days." During the twenty-two-month
cruise of the *Alabama*, Kell was off the ship for only a total
of twenty-two hours, less than any other man aboard her.

The crew were of different opinions regarding their "luff."
According to one alleged *Alabama* sailor, Kell was referred to
as "Kill-or-cure" by the crew. Another sailor wrote Kell years
after the war that he was "the only man we fellows on the
berth deck would fight or go to hell for. You were liked and
respected by all the crew." Still another seaman, a gunner's
mate, reminisced in later years: "Mr. Kell, you were kind and
good to us all, but we sure had to mind you and I'm glad
of it." An interesting observation is that made by Captain
Evan P. Jones of the yacht *Deerhound* shortly after the sinking
of the *Alabama*. Jones had the opportunity to observe a number
of officers and sailors from the raider after they had been
plucked from the water, and—aboard the yacht—were being
taken to Southampton. He noted: "Semmes seemed to be
greatly reverenced by his crew, but I think Kell had their deep-
est regard. According to their idea, Kell was Semmes' mainstay
and chief counsellor, and the commander owed much of his
success and reputation to his first officer's sagacity and prompt-
ness of resource."

But the opinion of an English sailor given just after the sinking of the *Alabama* was far different. He told a reporter: "As
a rule the crew liked and respected Semmes, but detested the

first lieutenant, who was a low lived bully, and a man without any principle." Kell, responsible as he was for maintaining discipline, could hardly have been popular with many of the sailors punished on his or on Semmes' orders, and this sailor could well have been among these men. Semmes himself said of his "luff": "You will scarcely recognize him . . . when you see him . . . on deck, arraigning some culprit 'at the mast' for a breach of discipline."

Regardless of how the crew may have felt toward him, Kell would later be loud in his praise of them. After the war, the stories of the *Alabama* and her crew that were critical of either would arouse Kell to a fury. He stated: "With our peculiar service, and with our ports locked against us, we were compelled to observe the strictest discipline, both with officers and crew. As the executive officer who enforced this discipline I may say that a nobler set of young men filling the position of officers, and a braver and more willing crew, never floated." Kell recalled: "Every day, whether it brought us a prize or not, had its duties. We were employed all the time. I was constantly putting the men through drills with small arms and with guns. . . . It was my duty to see that the crew and ship were in order at all times and I believe I did so."

If the accounts of captured Yankee mariners can be believed—and certainly these men had no love for Semmes or the Southern Confederacy—conditions on the *Alabama* were far from ideal. According to one such source:

> The sailors appeared like a lot of thieves, taking everything they could stow about their persons, and not appearing to take any notice of their officer, the officer himself not seeming to know much about a ship, except as regards the burning of her. . . . So little discipline was there that the Alabama's men were smoking segars [sic] in the boat that took the Captain on board the Alabama's decks. The men were lying about aft, as well as forward, smoking pipes and segars. . . . The ship was very dirty, and everything looking in disorder.

Without question there were skulkers and troublemakers among the crew, and discontent increased as the cruise lengthened. According to the English sailor who detested Kell, "There is no principle among the men, and very little enthusiasm in the cause." Later in Cherbourg, he would provide a news reporter with a "sour grapes" account of sailor life aboard the *Alabama*:

> Many of the men have been heavily fined by sentence of court martial. It has been a custom to punish the men sometimes for the most trivial offences by taking away their pay. On one occasion a man was fined five pounds for cutting a duck's throat taken out of a prize. Whenever we took a prize the officers always made a rush for all good eatables and drinkables, while the men were not allowed a single article, and severely punished if they touched anything. When the bread was full of maggots and the provisions in the *Alabama* of the very worst description, tons of the very best provisions, taken from prizes, have been sunk rather than give them to the men. Semmes' idea was this:—If he allowed men to take anything from a prize he supposed that the man who actually went to the prize would get it and keep it, without sharing with the others.

After a coaling stop at Fernando de Noronha in April, the *Alabama* arrived at Bahia on May 11. Two days later the C.S.S. *Georgia* arrived, commanded by William L. Maury. It was a "joyous experience" for Kell to meet old shipmates of the *Sumter*—Lieutenants William Evans and Robert Chapman. There was much news to exchange, and the *Alabama's* officers took particular delight in relating the details of their sinking of the *Hatteras*.

After ten days at Bahia, the *Alabama* was again at sea, and in the following weeks added to her growing list of captures.

On July 30 the *Alabama* arrived at Saldanha Bay, northwest of Cape Town, to undertake repairs and take on supplies. Again, the misconduct of the liberty men increased Kell's overload of work. One of the men went so far as to draw a revolver on one of the master's mates. After stopping all further liberty, Semmes admitted his low opinion of the "sailor class of the present day," of which he thought his men typical: "I have a precious set of rascals on board—faithless in the matter of abiding by their contracts, liars, thieves, and drunkards."

His only consolation lay in the fact they were not Southern men.

For Kell, after the tedious work of supervising and disciplining, came welcome relief from duty in an invitation from an admiring Boer to accompany him on an ostrich hunt in the interior. Armed with shotguns, Kell and his companions from the *Alabama* succeeded in shooting one of the birds, but their buckshot had no effect. Nevertheless, they enjoyed the day's diversion from ship duty. At Saldanha and the other stopovers near Cape Town, the officers and men of the *Alabama* were amazed and delighted at the admiration and praise they received. They were treated as heroes. Daily, throngs of friendly Boers came aboard the ship. Semmes, wearing an "old grey, stained uniform" with "battered shoulder straps", received the visitors in his cabin, where he was beseiged with requests for his autograph. He dismissed praise of his sinking of the *Hatteras* with the admission that "both in tonnage and in armament" that ship was "rather inferior to his own." Kell, proudly pointing out the Blakely gun for the special attention of visitors, remarked: "When we fought the *Hatteras* these conical shells struck her one after the other in capital style; they exploded with magnificent effect and lit up her whole broadside." One visitor expressed amazement at finding "so small a vessel carrying such large metal." A photographer from Cape Town, taking pictures of Semmes and his officers, included one of both with the impressive-looking gun. Kell would always remember the pro-Southern Boers who had provided the most cordial welcome ever accorded the *Alabama* and her officers. Both he and Semmes were given valuable ostrich feathers by admirers.

The *Alabama* next rounded the Cape of Good Hope and stopped at Simon's Bay for additional repairs. Semmes had become thoroughly disgusted by the conduct of his sailors. In spite of precautions, liquor was smuggled on board, and there was much insubordination. Worse still, as Semmes complained, "With one or two exceptions the whole crew have broken their liberty—petty officers and all. [My sailor] is as big a drunkard and as great a villain as ever." The captain

Captain Raphael Semmes standing by his ship's 110 pounder rifled gun. First Lieutenant John M. Kell is in the background in this photo taken at Capetown, South Africa in August, 1863.

knew better than to pay the bills presented against his men. When it came time to leave Simon's Bay, fourteen of the crew were missing (some, reportedly, at "Black Sophie's" bordello in Cape Town) and Semmes was compelled to impress "11 vagabonds, hungry and nearly shirtless" to replace them. It would take weeks to make sailors out of them, as well as to "work the grog" out of the rest of the crew before they settled down into "good habits and cheerfulness."

The *Alabama* next cruised between Africa and Brazil before returning to Simon's Bay. By this time, Semmes was feeling the pressing demands of duty. "Disgusted" with the sea, he felt it time to quit a life of "hardships and discomforts" suited only to "the youthful, or, at most, the middle-aged."

By late 1863, the Confederate raider, C.S.S. *Alabama* was on the other side of the globe, in the Indian Ocean. The *Alabama* was now encountering fewer American vessels, and Semmes believed that the trade "is nearly broken up. Their ships find it impossible to get freights." Semmes was tired and ill after over three years at sea. He admitted in his journal that he was "quite knocked up with cold and fever" and "supremely disgusted with the sea and all its belongings." Semmes longed for a chance to just "lie by and be quiet." His sailors were still causing trouble. After cigars, taken from the *Winged Racer*, were divided among the officers and crew, a number of the sailors threw theirs overboard "in a contemptuous manner." Semmes immediately had the "ringleaders" arrested, and, soon afterward, court-martialed. But this was only part of Semmes' discipline problem. The testimony of an officer of the clipper ship *Contest*—burned on November 11, 1863—gives an indication of how serious conditions aboard the *Alabama* may have been:

Crew much dissatisfied, no prize money, no liberty, and see no prospect of getting any. Discipline very slack, steamer dirty, rigging slovenly. Semmes sometimes punishes, but is afraid to push too hard. Men excited, officers do not report to captain, crew do things for which they would be shot on board American man-of-war; for instance, saw one of crew strike a master's mate;

Lieutenant Arthur Sinclair, Jr., (left) and Lieutenant R.F. Armstrong on deck during the *Alabama's* visit to Capetown, South Africa. The gun is a 32 pounder of Lieutenant Sinclair's division.

crew insolent to petty officers; was told by at least two-thirds
of them that [they] will desert on first opportunity. Crew all
scum of Liverpool, French, Dutch, etc. *Alabama* is very weak;
in any heavy sea her upper works leak badly; she has a list
to port that she may fight her starboard guns. Fires kept banked;
can get steam in 20 minutes. Except at muster no uniforms worn.
Crew rugged; keep a lookout at foretop-gallant yard daytime;
at night, two waist lookouts. Officers on duty have cutlass and
revolver; never saw Semmes in uniform; puts on sword at muster.
Have given up small-arm drill, afraid to trust crew with arms.
While on board saw drill only once, and that at pivot guns,
very badly done; men ill disposed and were forced to it; lots
of cursing.

On December 21 the *Alabama* arrived at New Harbour, a
short distance from the British colony of Singapore. They would
spend two days here taking on coal and provisions. The
Alabama's reputation was well known. When news of her arrival
began to circulate among the natives, there were excited exclamations of "Kappal Hantu!" ("Ghost Ship!")   On the 23rd
visitors were allowed on board, and the Confederate officers,
in dress uniform, proudly gave tours of their ship. Europeans
and natives alike crowded aboard. It was a friendly crowd,
and the Confederates were delighted with the goodwill and
support they received. The narrative of a British resident of
Singapore sharply contrasts with Northern accounts of the
deterioration of discipline. After a tour of the ship, he noted:

> I could remark no sign of impatience, much less of insubordina-
> tion. Nor could I attribute this contented behaviour to fear of
> the officers, who were far from rough or domineering in their
> manners; so that I conclude whatever may be their hardships
> or the precarious nature of their pay and emoluments, the crew
> of the *Alabama* would stand by her in case of danger.

The same British gentleman was also filled with praise for
the officers with whom he conversed. The latter admitted quite
frankly that capturing and destroying merchantmen was losing
its excitement for them, and the Britisher was left with the

feeling that they would eventually risk an encounter with an armed enemy ship. However, he concluded that Semmes was "a man slow to move on a rash enterprise."

When the *Alabama* arrived at New Harbour, eighteen American merchantmen were in port. However, within a few days of their arrival, about one-half had changed owners and were flying the flags of other nations. It was little wonder that one of the Confederates remarked: "We don't care much whether or not we succeed in destroying any more of the enemy's merchantmen; we have done enough already; our presence alone in these waters will now suffice to ruin the eastern commerce of the Federal States."

Proud of their record of accomplishments, the *Alabama* officers continued to be annoyed at denunciations in the Northern press of their alleged "piratical" activities. On this sensitive issue, they were especially anxious to present their own rebuttal. While at New Harbour, an officer explained:

You must remember, sir, that we but retaliate on our enemy that destruction of property which he has been the first to inaugurate in this war. His power at sea was by a simple chance too much for us to cope with from the first, or we should by this time have had a small navy of our own, built in our own dockyards; and as we have been content to fight him in the field with a disparity of numbers, so we should have attacked him at sea with a weaker force. Such has not been our fortune; but it has been our fortune to obtain this and some few other ships, and to bring them to bear on our enemies' most salient point. General Gilmore himself, when he uses the advantage which the Federal ships have placed in his hands to destroy from his batteries the warehouses and mansions of Charleston, endorses our course as legitimate. It is true, Charleston has its forts and batteries which do their best to protect these defenceless buildings, but does this alter the parallel? Is it confessed that the merchant shipping of the Federal Government can find no protection in the Federal navy? and if it is so confessed, is it urged that we should therefore hold back from the advantage which our enemies' defencelessness gives us in one particular, while he advantages to the full by our insufficiently protected state in another? No! When the Northern hordes pause on their onward raid by the consideration of the inability of the Confederate Government to afford protection to its cities, then may we too pause on our course, for the reason that the Federal Government cannot or will not spare ships from the blockade of Southern ports to protect her foreign shipping.

On the night of December 24, thirty miles out of New Harbour, the *Alabama* hailed the barque *Martaban*, flying the English flag. Despite the flag, she was believed to be American. As Kell would say, "We could tell them as infallibly by the 'cut of their jib' as we could detect by their sharp brogue the nationality of their captains." The captain, after producing British papers, insisted that his was an English ship. Claiming the protection of his flag, he refused to accompany the boarding party to the *Alabama*. For the first time, Semmes was forced to personally board a captured vessel. Declaring the ship's papers a forgery, he ordered that the barque be burned. Later, the skipper, aboard the *Alabama* and under oath, admitted that he had "tried a game of bluff." Two days later Semmes had destroyed two more ships—these undeniably American—but he was troubled at the possibility of adverse reaction to his burning of the *Martaban*. His prisoners were put adrift in longboats to make their way to New Harbour as best they could. With them Semmes sent a report which attempted to justify the destruction of the *Martaban*.

Early in 1864 the *Alabama* left the Indian Ocean and headed for European waters. Semmes noted in his journal on May 21: "Our bottom is in such a state that everything passes us. We are like a crippled hunter limping home from a long chase." During almost two years at sea, the *Alabama* had never been long enough in any port for a thorough overhaul of her hull, rigging, and engines. Since her fires had never been allowed to go out, flues and pipes had never been properly cleaned. On April 23 Semmes made a target of the prize *Rockingham*. Shot and shell were used—according to Semmes—"with reasonable success." Others thought differently. Of twenty-four rounds fired, only seven were seen to have any effect.

The prisoners from the *Rockingham* attributed this to bad shooting, but there were other possibilities, of which Kell gradually became aware. Upon investigation, he found that many of the shell fuses were faulty. It would later be found that a large quantity of powder had become damp because of the magazine's proximity to the condensing apparatus. Powder had so deteriorated that several barrels would have to be thrown overboard only a day before the action with the *Kearsarge*. Even the supply of powder put up in cartridges and stowed in copper tanks, which Semmes assumed was still in good condition, had—he would later admit—deteriorated, "perhaps to the extent of one-third of its strength." The size of the problem would not be known until weeks later. But there was no question that the *Alabama* needed to be put up in dry dock for repairs that would take at least a month. As Kell observed, the ship was "loose at every joint, her seams were open, and the copper on her bottom was in rolls."

At midday on June 11, 1864, the *Alabama* dropped anchor at Cherbourg, France. During her twenty-two months at sea, she had overhauled 294 vessels. Of this number, fifty-five American merchant ships (valued at over $4,500,000) had been burned and ten others (valued at $562,000) bonded. It was a record that would not be equalled by any other Confederate raider. The presence of the *Alabama* at Cherbourg was an embarrassment for the French authorities there. Since the docks were naval property, only Emperor Napoleon III—away on a vacation—could give the necessary permission for her to be docked. However, Semmes was allowed to land his prisoners and take on coal.

On June 14 the U.S.S. *Kearsarge,* commanded by John A. Winslow, appeared off the breakwater. Semmes had learned the day before of her coming and faced three alternatives: he could continue waiting for permission to dry-dock, he could leave Cherbourg at once without taking on coal, or he could fight. If he made the first choice, he would lose most of his crew, and the Federals would be waiting in greater strength for him to leave. And Semmes—who was actually spoiling for a fight—had no intention of making a getaway. His know-

U.S.S. *Kearsarge*

John A. Winslow, a Union naval officer during the Civil War. As captain of the U.S.S. *Kearsarge,* Winslow commanded the Union warship in the battle off Cherbourg.

ledge of the *Kearsarge* convinced him that his own ship was a match for her. When the *Kearsarge* steamed into view, Kell, glass in hand, stood on the quarter-deck trying to make out hull, rigging, and battery. He saw a "smooth black hull," but—since her principal guns were pivoted—he could learn little of her battery. However, Semmes believed he had adequate knowledge of the *Kearsarge,* since he had seen her at close range two years earlier at Gibraltar.

Soon after the arrival of the *Kearsarge,* Semmes summoned Kell to his cabin. He said:

> I have sent for you to discuss the advisability of fighting the *Kearsarge.* As you know, the arrival of the *Alabama* at this port has been telegraphed to all parts of Europe. Within a few days, Cherbourg will be effectively blockaded by Yankee cruisers. It is uncertain whether or not we shall be permitted to repair the *Alabama* here, and in the meantime, the delay is to our advantage. I think we may whip the *Kearsarge,* the two vessels being of wood and carrying about the same number of men and guns. Besides, Mr. Kell, although the Confederate States government has ordered me to avoid engagements with the enemy's cruisers, I am tired of running from that flaunting rag!

Kell was not really convinced that the decision to fight was a wise one, but—as he later admitted—he "could not remonstrate with Captain Semmes." Instead, he reminded him of their defective powder and of the fact that at target practice with the *Rockingham* only one in three fuses had been good. Semmes shrugged off Kell's concern, saying: "I will take the chances of one in three." There was nothing left for Kell to say except, "I'll fit the ship for action, sir." As he later wrote: "I saw his mind was fully made up, so I simply stated these facts for myself." Kell began ordering preparation of shell rooms, guns, and other equipment. Cutlasses and axes were sharpened for hand-to-hand combat, should a boarding take place. From the 15th to the 18th they took on coal, filling bunkers with a full load of three hundred and fifty tons. As for morale, Semmes noted in his journal:

> My crew seen to be in the right spirit, a quiet spirit of determination pervading both officers and men. The combat will no doubt be contested and obstinate, but the two ships are so equally matched that I do not feel at liberty to decline it. God defend the right, and have mercy upon the souls of those who fall, as many of us must.

Soon after the *Kearsarge* had arrived, Semmes had sent a message to Winslow (through the American consul at Cherbourg) of his intention to fight. He received no reply from Winslow, who had earlier been advised by Secretary of the Navy Gideon Welles: "To accept or send a challenge would be to recognize the pirates on terms of equality, elevating them and degrading our own." But Winslow had no intention of allowing the *Alabama* to escape. It was arranged with the American consul that men be stationed on the bluff overlooking the harbor. They were to fire signal rockets in the event that Semmes tried to leave port under cover of darkness.

By June 18 Semmes felt that his ship and crew were ready. He refused to be influenced by the "unanimous feeling" of the French port authorities, who advised that he should avoid

Gideon Welles, Secretary of the Navy under Lincoln. Welles advised Captain Winslow of the U.S.S. *Kearsarge* that challenging the C.S.S *Alabama* to battle would be an admission that the *Alabama* was more than a pirate ship.

combat with a "superior force." Semmes would write in his official report after the battle: "Mr. Kell, my first lieutenant, deserves great credit for the fine condition in which the ship went into action, with regard to her battery, magazine, and shell rooms." But when Captain George Terry Sinclair, Confederate naval agent in Europe, arrived at Cherbourg from Paris only hours before the battle, he found the *Alabama*'s officers looking "rough, jaded, and worn out." He observed of Semmes: "He seemed to have weighed the matter well in his own mind, and determination was marked in every line of his faded and worn countenance." Before disembarking, Sinclair advised Semmes to keep his ship at a respectful distance from Winslow's powerful 11-inch pivot guns.

Spectators on shore at Cherbourg, France watch the battle between the U.S.S. *Kearsarge* and C.S.S. *Alabama* on June 19, 1864.

4

Fight Off Cherbourg

Sunday, June 19, 1864. The day was bright and cloudless, with only a slight haze. On the *Alabama* the fires had been started shortly after 6 a.m. As Semmes inspected his men, dressed in clean white frocks and blue trousers, he commented on their smart looks. He also remarked to Lieutenant Sinclair, "If the bright, beautiful, day is shining for our benefit, we should be happy at the omen." The officers, in their best uniforms, were tense with excitement as they paced the decks. Decks and brass work were immaculate from recent holystoning and polishing, and overhead flew the Confederate ensign. Musing over his prospects, Semmes surprised his fifth lieutenant by asking, "How do you think it will turn out today, Mr. Sinclair?" Sinclair, unaccustomed to being consulted by his captain, replied: "I cannot answer the question, sir, but can assure you the crew will do their full duty, and follow you to the death." Semmes replied, "Yes, that's true," and began his pacing of the quarter-deck.

Kell continued to be the busiest officer aboard, as he supervised the final preparations for battle. The decks were sanded and tubs of water were placed along the spar deck as a precaution against fire. Then the men were sent to their stations, apparently convinced that the *Kearsarge* would be as easy to defeat as the *Hatteras* had been.

At about 9:45 a.m. the *Alabama* got under way. She passed in front of the French ironclad frigate *Couronne*, which had started her own fires hours earlier. The *Couronne* would escort the Confederate raider to the three-mile limit to make certain that there was no violation of French territory. As the *Alabama* passed the liner *Napoleon*, the crew of the French vessel manned the rigging and gave three rousing cheers, then their band broke out with "Dixie." Thousands of spectators—Confederate and Union sympathizers alike—were arrayed upon the hillsides, on the breakwater, atop buildings, and aboard vessels. Among those situated to watch the fight were Englishman John Lancaster and his family, vacationing aboard their private yacht *Deerhound*. That morning at breakfast the family had held a vote to determine whether to attend church services or watch the fight from their yacht. The children all elected to see the action. In addition to the *Couronne* and the *Deerhound*, a few pilot and fishing boats trailed along. Aboard one pilot boat was the artist Edouard Manet, equipped with pencils, colors, and sketchbook. Manet would produce one of the most accurate representations of the *Alabama-Kearsarge* engagement. The Cherbourg photographer, Rondin, had brought his equipment onto the old church tower overlooking the harbor, and he would attempt to photograph the fight.

After the *Alabama* steamed around the breakwater and sighted the *Kearsarge*, three miles away, Semmes headed his ship directly toward the enemy. The starboard battery was prepared for action. Semmes ordered Kell to have all hands piped aft, and, when they had gathered, he had his secretary read them a prepared speech. Semmes had prepared his speech with great care, for he wanted to arouse the men. Breedlove Smith read:

Officers and Seamen of the Alabama: You have, at length, another opportunity of meeting the enemy—the first that has been presented to you since you sank the *Hatteras!* In the meantime you have been all over the world, and it is not too much to say, that you have destroyed, and driven for protection under neutral flags, one half of the enemy's commerce, which, at the beginning of the war, covered every sea. This is an achievement of which you may well be proud; and a grateful country will not be unmindful of it. The name of your ship has become a household

word wherever civilization extends! Shall that name be tarnished
by defeat? The thing is impossible! Remember that you are in
the English Channel, the theatre of so much of the naval glory
of our race, and that the eyes of all Europe are at this moment,
upon you. The flag that floats over you is that of a young Republic,
who bids defiance to her enemies, whenever and wherever
found! Show the world that you know how to uphold it! Go
to your quarters.

The sailors cheered enthusiastically, shouting "Never! Never!"
at mention of defeat. One of their number, in a later interview,
stated the reason for their optimism:

> The crew fully expected from the beginning that they would
> be led by Captain Semmes close alongside the Kearsarge so as
> to commence the action at close quarters and finish by boarding
> her. It was expected that Semmes would lead the boarders in
> person, for though we had as fine a crew as any ship afloat,
> yet we had not a single competent gunner on board, excepting
> the captain of the forward pivot, a hundred pound rifle gun.
> He was an old English man of war man, trained in the British
> navy. The captains of the other guns were not competent gunners,
> though brave men.

The sailors returned to their quarters, where they stripped
to the waist and were allowed to smoke and rest to reserve
their strength.

Aboard the *Kearsarge* shortly after 10 a.m., the signal bell
had just summoned the men for divine service. Captain Winslow, wearing a rather rusty-looking uniform, was opening his
Bible when the lookout gave the cry, "Here she comes! The
Alabama!" Winslow closed the Bible and told a cabin boy to
bring up his side arms. He ordered the drummer to sound
quarters. James Wheeler, acting master, ran to the hatchway
of the wardroom mess and shouted to the startled officers
below, "She's coming! She's coming, and heading straight for
us!" Within two minutes all the men were at their stations.
It is likely that they recalled Winslow's remark of three days
earlier: "My lads, I will give you one hour to take the *Alabama*,
and I think you can do it!" He had also warned them, "Semmes

Acting Master James R. Wheeler (left) and Assistant Engineer Sidney L. Smith standing by the U.S.S. *Kearsarge's* forward 11 inch pivot gun in June, 1864.

is a tricky man and may try another *Hatteras* game on us."
Running on a full head of steam, the *Kearsarge* was turned
northeastward to open sea. Winslow wanted the battle to be
fought well outside the three-mile limit both to avoid any incident with the French authorities and to prevent Semmes from
escaping. Aware that he would have a greater advantage at
close range, he ordered his guns loaded with five-second shell
and sighted for five hundred yards.

After reaching the three-mile limit, the *Couronne* turned and
left the *Alabama,* which was still headed toward the *Kearsarge.*
Meanwhile, the *Kearsarge* had moved seven miles out to sea
before turning around. Then, as the two vessels steamed
directly at each other, the decks of the *Kearsarge* were sanded.
Winslow's plan was to run down the *Alabama* or, "if circum-
stances did not warrant it, to close in with her."

Semmes, standing on the horse block, the highest point on
deck, had his glasses trained on the *Kearsarge.* His two pivot
guns were rotated to starboard, as he intended to engage the
enemy on that side. Semmes realized that the two 11-inch
Dahlgrens on the *Kearsarge* gave the Federals an advantage
at close range, while his own 100-pound Blakely pivot gun
was most effective at long range. He had it set for two thousand
yards and loaded with solid shot. Lieutenant Armstrong—commanding the gun—was instructed to have his gunners aim
low—at the hull of the *Kearsarge.* Better to fire too low than
too high, Semmes told his men, as the ricochet of their shot
over the smooth water would remedy any defect in their vertical
aim.

It was now about 11 a.m.,   forty-five minutes since they
had rounded the breakwater. When a mile and a quarter's
distance from the *Kearsarge,* the *Alabama* sheered, discharging
her Blakely. The shot went high. The *Kearsarge,* on full steam,
came with such speed that the *Alabama* was able to discharge
only two more shot, which were also too high and damaged
only the rigging.

Suddenly Winslow sheered off, presenting his starboard battery. The men responded instantly to his order: "All the divi-
sions! Aim low for the waterline! Fire! Load and fire as rapidly

The U.S.S. Kearsarge opens the fight with C.S.S. Alabama off Cher-bourg, France on June 19, 1864.

as possible!" The thirty-pound rifle gun on the topgallant forecastle, manned by the marine detachment, was the first fired. A shell struck the *Alabama* near her forward port, throwing out splinters and wounding a man at a gun. A sailor later recalled: "He leaped away with a leg smashed, and another man at the next gun fell dead. The shell caught our slide rack, and I think the man was killed by one of our own shot, which was thrown against him by the shell of the *Kearsarge*." The *Alabama* next received a full broadside. Winslow intended to run under the *Alabama's* stern, but Semmes' keeping his broadside exposed prevented this. At five hundred yards, both ships were forced into a circular track under full steam, moving in opposite directions and each fighting her starboard side. The positions of the ships reminded one Yankee sailor of "two flies crawling around on the rim of a saucer." They would make seven complete circles before the end of the action, gradually lessening the distance between them by about a hundred yards.

The action was now continuous on both sides. An assistant engineer on the deck of the *Kearsarge* was able to see shot and shell from the *Alabama* "skip like stones . . . thrown to ricochet until they burst to windward with a hollow roar, sending aloft a shower of glittering spray." The *Alabama* fired at least two shots for every one of the *Kearsarge.* Although Kell believed that his men "handled their guns beautifully," he would also give due credit to his adversary: "She came into action magnificently." The "luff" was standing near the eight-inch pivot gun commanded by Lieutenant Wilson, when suddenly an 11-inch shell exploded through the gun port and—as Kell later recalled—wiped out "like a sponge from a blackboard one-half of the gun's crew." A second shell killed one man and injured others. Then a third shell from the *Kearsarge* struck the breast of the gun carriage and spun around on deck without exploding. Seaman Mars, compressor man, quickly picked it up and threw it over the side. Lieutenant Wilson, in a state of shock at being struck by blood and limbs, was in no condition to continue his command. Mars signalled to Kell, requesting permission to clear the deck. Kell bowed

Acting Master Eben M. Stoddard (left) and Chief Engineer William H. Cushman standing by the U.S.S. ***Kearsarge's*** **after 11 inch pivot gun, in June, 1864. Note the shell and grape shot on deck by the gun.**

his head in assent, and the remains were shoveled into the sea.   After the deck had been re-sanded, the places of Wilson and the dead and wounded were filled on Kell's order by Midshipman Anderson and eight men from a nearby thirty-two-pound gun. They worked coolly and methodically.

About twenty minutes after the action began, the spanker gaff that flew the *Alabama*'s colors was shot away, and the flag fell to just above the deck. Another flag was immediately raised at the mizzenmast head. At about the same time, a shell from the *Alabama* struck the hull of the *Kearsarge*. The men on the *Alabama* cheered, believing they had "knocked her engines to pieces," before they realized there had been no damage. With a "look of astonishment on his face," Semmes turned to his chief officer: "Mr. Kell, our shells strike the enemy's side, doing little damage, and fall into the water. Try solid shot."   This was done, and later both shot and shell were used alternately.

Positioned on the horse block to best direct the maneuvering of the ship, Semmes left his gunners with "no particular orders" during the action.   However, it was later claimed by his sailors that he offered a reward to the men who could silence the two 11-inch guns that were causing such havoc aboard his ship. During the fight Semmes is reported to have said of his opponents: "Confound them, they've been fighting twenty minutes, and they're cool as posts."

Kell distinguished himself throughout, and Semmes later praised his "coolness and judgement."   Another officer later recalled Kell's behavior during the fight:

Nothing could exceed the cool and thorough attention to details of our first lieutenant. . . . From point to point of the spar-deck in his rapid movement he was directing here, or advising there; now seeing to the transfer of shot, shell, or cartridge; giving his orders to this and that man or officer, as though on dress-muster; occasionally in earnest conversation with Semmes, who occupied the horse-block, glasses in hand, and leaning on the hammock-rail; at times watching earnestly the enemy, and then casting his eye about our ship, as though keeping a careful reckoning of the damage given and received. Nothing seemed

The battle between C.S.S. *Alabama* and U.S.S. *Kearsarge* on June 19, 1864 off the coast of Cherbourg, France.

to escape his active mind or eye, his commanding figure at all times towering over the heads of those around.

Aboard the *Kearsarge*, Captain Winslow stood atop an arms chest on the starboard side of the quarter-deck, half of his body exposed above the rail, as he overlooked his own deck while scrutinizing the enemy. He repeatedly gave the order, "Faster, sir! Faster! Four bells!" to his third engineer, while holding up four fingers signifying "Full speed ahead!"   He gave orders in the same manner to Quartermaster William Poole at the helm. In addition to his other duties, Winslow watched the oncoming shells, directing the men near him when to dodge them. Other officers were also warning their gun crews when to drop to the deck. Men would drop flat, supporting themselves on hands and toes until the shot had struck or gone "howling" by, then spring up to resume action. Seaman John Bickford, working the pivot gun, had a shell pass so close that the air suction caused him to gasp. When his gun captain asked why he had not dodged it, he answered, between gasps, "Haven't time, sir. I'm busy." Cheer after cheer rent the air as shot and shell poured into the *Alabama*. There were exclamations of "That is a good one!" "Down boys—give her another like the last!" "That's for the pirates!" as the men calmly and precisely worked the guns.   Drenched in sweat and covered with powder stains, they were alternately laughing, talking, and cheering. The sponger of one gun was so stained with a "thick coating of burnt powder that it was hard to tell where blue undershirt ended and skin began." Kell's counterpart on the *Kearsarge*—Executive Officer James S. Thornton—passed from one gun to another, advising the crews: "Don't fire unless you get good aim; one shot that hits is better than fifty thrown away."   There was a brief pause in the action at one of the pivot guns as both vessels became enveloped in smoke. To an officer's anxious inquiry as to the cause of the delay, a gun captain replied, "Nothing is the matter, sir. She is all ready to give him a dose." "Then why in hell don't you fire?" demanded the officer. "I'll fire, sir, as soon as I get sight," came the unruffled reply. The smoke soon disappeared, and a missile from the gun struck the ocean close to the *Alabama*'s water line, sending a shower of spray into the air.   There was even comic relief for the Federals. To the amusement of their shipmates, two old sailors used up a box of ammunition firing a 12-pound howitzer boat gun.

Among the many observers on shore was Captain Sinclair. Equipped with "splendid glasses," Sinclair noted that, although the *Alabama* fired three shots for every two of her opponent, she usually fired too high. He also noticed a difference in the powder smoke of the two ships: that from the *Alabama* resembled "puffs of heavy steam," while that of the *Kearsarge* was "much lighter."   It was obvious to those taking part in the action that there was a difference. As Kell later recalled, "The report from the *Kearsarge*'s battery was clear and sharp, the powder burning like thin vapor, while our guns gave out a dull report, with thick and heavy vapor." Thus was Kell proved correct in his earlier evaluation of the condition of the *Alabama*'s powder and the extent of its deterioration. The situation was far more serious than Semmes had believed at the time he sent his challenge to Winslow.

There was no question, moreover, as to the superiority of the gunners on the *Kearsarge*. Kell would admit that the Yankee guns were "served beautifully, being aimed with precision, and deliberate in fire."   One well qualified to know about the *Alabama* and her crew was Commander Bulloch. He would write that her sailors "had not been trained to judge of distances, and were wholly without the skill, precision and coolness which come only with practice and the habit of firing at a visible object and noting the effect."   Captain Winslow noted in his official report: "The firing of the *Alabama* from the first was rapid and wild. Toward the close of the action her firing became better." An *Alabama* sailor admitted: "Our guns were too much elevated, and shot over the *Kearsarge*. The men all fought well, but the gunners did not know how to point and elevate the guns."   A marine corporal on the *Kearsarge* noted the effect of this on the morale of the Federals:

When the battle commenced it made our hair stick right up

strait but after we had got settled down to work and saw by their rapid and haphazard fire that they were not doing us much damage we took it easy; they would fire when they were in their smoke and when we were enveloped in ours.

The corporal also observed that in their haste and excitement, the *Alabama*'s gunners fired off about six of their ramrods, resembling "black meteors with their long tails." Of the more than three hundred shot and shell fired by the Alabama during the hour-long engagement,   only twenty-eight struck the *Kearsarge,* and none of these did any significant damage. On the Federal side, the *Kearsarge* fired 173 shot and shell (mostly shell), a large number finding their mark and accounting for the "fearful work" of destruction. No grape or canister was used, although Winslow had a large quantity on hand.

Although the shells of the *Kearsarge* were taking a heavy toll in killed and wounded, the *Alabama* remained on the offensive, her captain waiting for the lucky shot that would cripple his opponent. At length, his forward pivot gun crew sent a 100-pound shell smashing under the counter of the *Kearsarge,* glancing along until it lodged in the rudderpost. As the *Kearsarge* trembled from the shock, the sailors on the *Alabama* cheered loudly. Here was their lucky shot. However, their cheers died when the anticipated explosion failed to occur. For Semmes and Kell, the failure was bitter; to his dying day each would believe that faulty powder or a defective fuse had prevented the shell from exploding. They were convinced that this shell alone could have sunk the *Kearsarge.* At the very least, they believed, it should have made the rudder inoperable and thus influenced the outcome, since the *Alabama* was still very much in the action.   Actually, however, if the shell had exploded at first contact—when it was supposed to—it would have damaged the ship's counter, some twenty feet from the sternpost.

John Bickford, a first loader on the *Kearsarge,* had a different version of the failure of so many shells to explode: "It's true that quite a number failed to explode, but it wasn't the fault of the shells. It was the fault of the excited men who fired them." According to Bickford, almost all of the unexploded shells from the *Alabama* still had on the lead caps which should have been ripped off by the gun loaders, as Bickford himself was doing. As he explained, unless the lead cap was removed to expose the fuse primer—set to explode in so many seconds—it was impossible for a shell to explode. The Yankee from Gloucester, Massachusetts—afterward awarded the Medal of Honor for "marked coolness and good conduct" during the fight—told of his experience with a shell he identified as Semmes' "lucky shot":

I was standing on the starboard side of the gun, with my foot directly on the planksheer, when all of a sudden I heard the whir of a shell, a Blakely, and instantly my foot got a jar that seemed to fill it with pins and needles. That sixty-eight pound [*sic*] shell had struck the planksheer and gone way through it, at least so far that it exposed its primer, or where it should be, but I saw that the patch was still there on the shell, and I knew that it never could explode, that it was just as harmless as a solid shot would be in a like situation.

Well, of course all the gun crew jumped back, looking for an explosion. I just turns round and says to 'em, "Never mind that, boys, it won't go off, because they forgot to take the patch off." I stayed where I was, loading the gun, and all the fellows jumped right to work again.

A shell from the *Alabama*'s Blakely gun caused the only casualties on the *Kearsarge*. It passed through the starboard bulwarks below the main rigging, exploding on the quarterdeck and injuring three sailors at the after pivot gun. William Gowin, the most seriously injured, refused assistance and dragged himself to the forward hatch, where he was helped below by the surgeon.

The twenty-eight shot and shell which struck the *Kearsarge* did no major damage. Twelve struck the hull, while eight were believed to have damaged the rigging. Two of the boats were put out of commission and one of the sails was badly torn. A shell entered the funnel of the *Kearsarge* and exploded, tearing out a space about three feet in diameter and throwing metal about the deck. A piece of the shell passed through the dipper of a thirsty fireman who had just raised it to his lips. For a moment the funnel appear to be falling as it rocked to and fro. A 100-pound shell ploughed across the roof of the engine room skylight, coming within fourteen inches of Engineer McConnell before passing harmlessly overboard through the port rail.

During the latter part of the fight, the *Alabama* received the full effect of accurate and deadly fire. Seaman James Hart, carrying a shell to his gun, was blown to pieces. The "first serious disaster" to the ship was the destruction of her rudder. For the remainder of the action, steering could be done only by using tackles. At about the same time—forty-five minutes after the battle had commenced—an 11-inch shell passed through the starboard side, emerging and exploding on her port side and tearing great gaps in her timbers and planking. To the exuberant *Kearsarge* sailors, it "raised the very devil." A coal bunker bulkhead caved in, filling the fire room and almost burying the men under coal. With only two boilers left working, the *Alabama*'s steam pressure was greatly reduced.

Filled with smoke and steam and with gaping holes in her hull, the *Alabama*—careening heavily to starboard—was in no condition to continue fighting. It was either escape, surrender, or be destroyed. The men were ordered to lie low, as it was feared that Winslow would now order a raking fire. But Semmes was not ready to surrender. He believed that by shifting the weight of his battery from starboard to port he might raise the shot holes above the water line. The ship was now five miles from the coast and with luck might make the three-mile limit. He gave the order: "Mr. Kell, as soon as our head points to the French coast in our circuit of action, shift your guns to port and make all sail for the coast." The helm was righted, the fore trysail sheets and two jibs hoisted, and the evolution executed successfully. At the same time, the pivot guns—after being cleared of the dead—were shifted to port with only a brief pause in the action. Kell appeared at the skylight above the engine room, and in a "voice of thunder" ordered the men below: "What is the matter in the engine room? Put on steam!'' Engineers Brooks and O'Brien, covered with sweat and coal dust, answered that the *Alabama* carried all the steam she could manage without blowing up. Then reconsidering, O'Brien declared, ''Let her have the steam; we had better blow her to hell than to let the Yankees whip us!'' But it would take more than the extra twenty-five pounds of steam to save the *Alabama*. Winslow had anticipated Semmes' intentions and steamed across his adversary's bow. He was now in a position to rake her.

Aboard the *Alabama*, none could doubt the seriousness of the situation. An officer, looking out a port and seeing the water rushing into the gangway at every roll, was certain that the *Alabama*'s ''last moments were close at hand.'' A sailor later recalled: ''Our men were then very fatigued and many disabled and wounded. We still fired as well as possible from the port side, though we knew the day was lost.'' Seaman John Roberts, who had been ordered by Kell to loose the jib, had executed the order and was returning to the deck when he was struck by a shell in the lower abdomen. With his entrails protruding, he succeeded in reaching the deck and was stumbling toward his gun when he fell dead. O'Brien came on deck to report that the rapidly rising water was almost flush with the furnace fires. He found Semmes on the horse block with a handkerchief tied around his hand to cover a painful although superficial wound. Semmes listened in silence, then replied: ''Return to your duty!'' The engineers were now certain that they would go down with the ship. Engineer Pundt said bitterly: ''Well, I suppose Old Beeswax has made up his mind to drown us like a lot of rats! Here, Matt! Take off my boots!'' On deck there was some confusion, ''though nothing like a panic, excepting on the part of one or two.''

For the second time the Confederate colors were shot away, this time falling to the deck. There was now some confusion aboard the *Alabama*—and a misunderstanding aboard the *Kearsarge*—possibly due to the erroneous belief that Semmes had surrendered. Semmes ordered Kell to find out how long the ship could float. Going below, Kell found the sight ''appalling.'' The holes in the hull were ''large enough to admit a wheel barrow." Surgeon Llewellyn was at his post, but the wounded man on his table had been swept away by a shell. Kell returned to the deck and reported that the ship could not remain afloat for more than ten minutes. Semmes gave the order: "Then, sir, cease firing, shorten sail, and haul down the colors; it will never do in this nineteenth century for us to go down, and the decks covered with our gallant wounded." As there was no white flag available, two men on the spanker boom held up a makeshift one—the white portion of the Confederate ensign. The officers and men on the *Kearsarge* would later claim that when they observed the white flag and the firing of a lee gun they ceased firing, but that two more shots were fired from the *Alabama*, one from the forward pivot gun. Unconvinced that his enemy had surrendered, Winslow cried out: "Give it to them again, boys; they are playing us a trick!" Each of his gun captains obeyed the order instantly, firing five volleys into the *Alabama*. Two 11-inch shells struck the coal bunker, throwing up coal dust as high as the yardarm. Aboard the doomed raider, Kell cried out: "Stand to your quarters, men. If we must be sunk after our colors are down, we will go to the bottom with every man at his post!" And among the sailors the word was passed, "There's no quarter for us!" But when the white flag was again raised on the spanker boom, all firing ceased. Semmes then ordered Kell: "Dispatch an officer to the *Kearsarge* and ask that they send boats to save our wounded—ours are disabled."

Finding the dinghy undamaged, Kell put Master's Mate Fullam in charge of her with instructions to surrender the ship and request assistance. Marine officer Howell, a nonswimmer, was allowed to take an oar as one of the crew. When Kell discovered that one boat was only slightly disabled, he directed the removal of the wounded to it. Among these was Seaman James King—"Connemara"— a troublemaker who had caused Kell many a headache since shipping on the *Alabama* at Singapore. As Kell stood briefly over the mortally wounded sailor, King seized his hand and kissed it. Amazed, Kell could not help thinking of the numerous times King had been punished on his orders.   Lieutenant Wilson and Dr. Galt were placed in charge of the boat and the wounded taken away, for the ship was settling fast. Winslow—who remembered how the *Hatteras* had been lured to destruction by Semmes—was apparently uncertain whether the *Alabama* was actually sinking. He continued to wait for more evidence. Only after Fullam had come aboard (after first deliberately dropping his sword over the side of the dinghy), was Winslow aware of the situation. Fullam delivered his message, then looking up and down the deck, asked where the dead and wounded were. When told that only three men had been wounded, he exclaimed, "My God, and it's a slaughter house over there!"   (He would later be astonished to learn that only nine men had been killed on the *Alabama* during the combat.) When Lieutenant Wilson came on board the *Kearsarge,* his appearance confirmed Fullam's account of the "slaughter" on the *Alabama*. He was covered with blood from the casualties at his gun early in the fight, and he still believed that sixteen of the seventeen men of his gun crew had been killed. Wilson offered Winslow his sword, but Winslow graciously refused it.

Aboard the sinking vessel Kell gave the order to abandon ship and directed the men to find a spar or whatever else might assist them in keeping afloat. As the men stripped to their underwear, Kell urged them over the side. He then returned to the stern, where Semmes, Bartelli, and a few other sailors were preparing to abandon ship. They were almost level with the ocean. Seaman Mars assisted Semmes as he removed his coat and boots, while the sail maker, Henry Alcott, helped Kell to pull off his boots. In the brief moment it took to do this, Kell recalled that on numerous occasions he had had Alcott punished for infractions of discipline.   Semmes still wore his cap (turned inside out), trousers, and vest, while Kell had stripped to his shirt and underdrawers. Both men had unceremoniously discarded their swords while undressing. Seaman Mars—one of the best swimmers on the ship—was entrusted with Semmes' papers (dispatches and accounts). Unfortunately, no one knew that Bartelli, who remained at his Captain's side, could not swim. It was now every man for himself. Wearing a life preserver, Semmes slipped into the sea, followed by Kell, who held onto a grating for support. The water "was like ice, and after the excitement of battle it seemed doubly cold." The men swam off as best they could to escape the vortex of the sinking ship. As the *Alabama* "settled stern foremost, launching her bows high in the air," Kell turned for a final look. He later recalled his feelings at the sight:

> As the gallant vessel, the most beautiful I ever beheld, plunged down to her grave, I had it on my tongue to call to the men who were struggling in the water to give three cheers for her, but the dead that were floating around me and the deep sadness I felt at parting with the noble ship that had been my home so long deterred me.

Kell's grating was not adequate, and he found the waves breaking over his head "distressingly uncomfortable." He later recalled: "I felt my strength giving out, but strange to say I never thought of giving up, though the white caps were breaking wildly over my head, and the sea foam from the billows blinding my eyes." Noticing a makeshift float of empty shell boxes, Kell shouted to a sailor, a good swimmer, to examine it. The man called out: "It is the doctor, sir, dead." Llewellyn, like Bartelli, was unable to swim, a fact of which his shipmates were unaware. Eight others also drowned before help came. Even good swimmers like Kell found it difficult to remain afloat. Seeing his senior officer weakening, Midshipman Maffitt began to disengage his life preserver, gasping out, "Mr. Kell, you are so exhausted, take this life preserver." Kell, however, knowing that the boy was prepared to sacrifice himself, refused. After what seemed like hours, but was actually only about thirty minutes, Kell heard a voice cry out, "Here's our Luff!" An *Alabama* sailor in one of the *Deerhound's* boats had recognized the expansive beard floating on the water. Kell was seized by the back of his neck and lifted into the boat.

Together with several of his crew, Semmes had already been rescued by the boat from Lancaster's yacht. Stretched out in

The surrender of the C.S.S. *Alabama* to the U.S.S. *Kearsarge* off Cherbourg.

the stern sheets "as pallid as death," he opened his eyes and gave his uninjured hand to Kell, who inquired, "Are you hurt?" "A little," came the answer. The hand injury was indeed slight, but he was suffering from exhaustion.   They were brought immediately to the *Deerhound*, where Kell learned the identity of the yacht and its owner. To Kell's surprise, he found Fullam aboard her. Winslow had allowed him to pick up survivors, and by not returning to the *Kearsarge*, the master's mate had cheated the Federals of several prisoners, including Howell, the brother-in-law of the Confederate President. From Fullam came the report that the *Kearsarge* had been protected by "chain armor". He had seen the places where the *Alabama*'s shot had torn the cover planking away, indenting and breaking the chain beneath.

The rescued men were made comfortable. Semmes had the jacket of an English lieutenant loaned him by Lancaster, while Kell wore that gentleman's carpet slippers and a pair of his trousers. Lancaster asked Semmes to what part of France he wished to be taken. He smiled at the reply, "Oh, any part of Great Britain."

As the Confederate raider settled stern first, Lieutenant Thornton aboard the *Kearsarge* passed the word, "Silence, boys."   Seaman Bickford told his gun crew that one could yell when licking a man "but not when you had him down." The reaction of one Yankee sailor was recorded in his journal:

> I was glad to see her go down and still I felt sorry for the poor fellows. It was a hard fight to see the poor fellows struggling in the water, some of them badly wounded, but still clinging to everything that they could lay their hands on to support themselves until our boats got near enough to pick them up.

As the Federals began rescuing the men still in the water, some, it was later claimed by *Kearsarge* sailors, would deliberately throw up their hands to avoid rescue. Only by the use of boat hooks were some of these men taken alive.   On board the *Kearsarge*, frightened prisoners gazed up in terror at the main yardarm, claiming that Semmes had warned them they

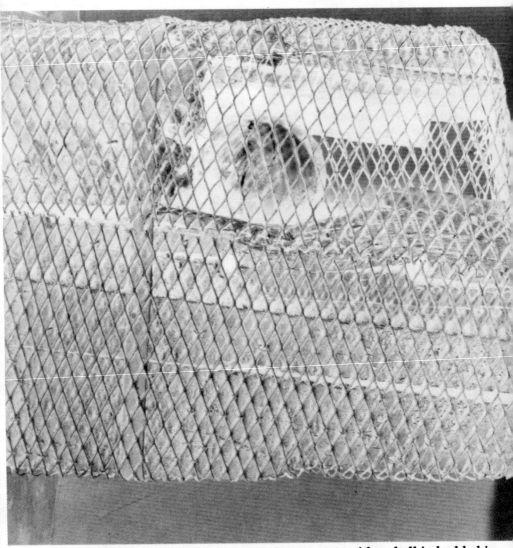

A section of the U.S.S. *Kearsarge's* sternpost, with a shell imbedded in it. The shell was fired by C.S.S. *Alabama* during the action off Cherbourg on June 19, 1864. The shell, from a rifled gun, is about 7 inches in diameter.

would be hung as pirates if captured. Much to their relief, they learned they were prisoners of war and would be treated humanely.   One *Alabama* sailor, mistaking Winslow for the ship's steward, asked him for whiskey. Identifying himself, Winslow gave him some whiskey and added, "My man, I am sorry for you." And pointing to his colors, he said, "That is the flag you should have been under."   Not all the men on the *Kearsarge*, however, had good will in their hearts. One sailor had an old score to settle with Semmes. George Whipple, formerly of the *Sumter*, had never forgiven him the punishment he had received aboard that vessel. Whipple crouched on the topgallant forecastle holding a Sharp's rifle, as he waited expectantly for Semmes to be brought on board. Discovered by some of his shipmates, he told them, "Captain Semmes shall never come on board this ship alive." Unsuccessful in persuading Whipple to give up his plan, the men finally reported him to an officer, who had the rifle seized.   Among the bodies brought aboard the *Kearsarge* was that of William Robinson, the carpenter, who had been Whipple's shipmate aboard the *Sumter*. Robinson had drowned, apparently because his drawers had slipped down around his ankles, exhausting him in the water.   Whipple was "much affected" by the death of the man who had nursed him to health after his ordeal on the *Sumter*.

Suddenly, the *Deerhound* was observed to be "stealing away." Bob Strahan, captain of a thirty-two-pounder, turned his gun directly upon her.   However, Winslow sent an officer to order him not to fire. As the *Deerhound* steamed away, the men waited in vain for the order to stop her. Years after the war, Executive Officer Thornton told an interviewer:

I was waiting impatiently for the order to come to fire on the English yacht which had rescued Semmes from his sinking ship. I never for a moment doubted that such an order would be given. But it was not, and I felt so indignant that I almost lost self-control. I felt for awhile that it was a barren victory and that we had spent our powder all for nothing.

Officers of the U.S.S. *Kearsarge* pose by her forward 11 inch Dahlgren pivot gun at Sydney, Australia in 1869.

Winslow later claimed he did not know the *Deerhound* was escaping; he refused at first to believe she could be "guilty of so disgraceful an act." Although there is no reason to doubt Winslow's statement, the ship's surgeon declared, "Probably not another person on board the *Kearsarge* was of the same opinion.... Captain Winslow alone is responsible for the escape of Semmes."

Winslow was generous in victory. Calling his sailors to muster, he read them a prayer and announced: "We have won the battle without loss of life; God must have been on our side. The *Alabama*'s men have been in the water, and you are requested to give them some of your clothing and report any expense to me. These men have surrendered; I want you to use them as brother shipmates. Your dinner will be served out to you. Share it with them." When the grog tub was brought up, all were allowed to refresh themselves.

Meanwhile, as the *Deerhound* steamed toward Southampton, the Confederates on board felt thankful they had been saved from death or imprisonment. When the officers tried to thank Lancaster, he merely told them, "Gentlemen, you have no need to give me any special thanks; I should have done exactly the same for the other people if they had needed it."

Upon their arrival at Southampton on the evening of the 19th, Semmes and Kell checked into the Kelway Hotel. Received in royal style, they were assigned rooms recently occupied by a prince. They found themselves the center of attention. Throughout the city the *Alabama-Kearsarge* battle was being discussed, and few Englishmen were disparaging the *Alabama*, considered a gallant underdog. Publicly, Semmes said nothing to credit Winslow his victory. He continually stressed the fact that he had been "completely deceived" as to the strength and armament of the *Kearsarge*. Had he known that she was "iron-clad" and more heavily armed than the *Alabama*, he said, he would not have fought; for him to have done so would have been "madness." An English reporter observed that

The C.S.S. *Sumter's* officers are shown in this engraving.

Semmes seemed to "be laboring under mental anguish and to feel most acutely the complete defeat he had experienced and the death and sufferings which that defeat had caused."

On June 30 orders were issued in Paris by Confederate Commander Samuel Barron for the officers of the *Alabama* to return to the Confederacy. Those taken prisoner by the *Kearsarge* had been paroled (except for Chief Engineer Freeman) along with the crew. Not all would return immediately, but on July 9 at Liverpool, Kell and Dr. Galt boarded the English mail steamer *Europa*, bound for Halifax.

It had been a sad parting for Kell and the officers and men of the *Alabama*. The great adventure had ended. Semmes would travel to the Continent for his health and would return to the Confederacy later.

Selected Bibliography

Books and Periodicals

Ammen, Daniel. *The Old Navy and the New*. Philadelphia: J. B. Lippincott, 1891.

Bennett, Frank M. *The Steam Navy of the United States: A History of the Growth of the Steam Vessel of War in the U.S. Navy, and of the Naval Engineer Corps*. Pittsburgh: W. T. Nicholson, 1896.

Bradlee, Francis Boardman Crowninshield. "The *Kearsarge-Alabama* Battle; The Story as told to the Writer by James Magee of Marblehead, Seaman on the *Kearsarge*," *Historical Collections of the Essex Institute*, LVII (1921).

Bradlow, Edna and Frank. *Here Comes the Alabama; the Career of a Confederate Raider*. Cape Town: A. A. Balkena, 1958.

Branham, Alfred Iverson. *Story of the Sinking of the Alabama 290: Interview with Capt. John McIntosh Kell, executive officer of the Alabama, given to Alfred Iverson Branham, forty-six years ago, June, 1883*. Atlanta: Cornell, 1930.

Browne, John M. "The Duel Between the *Alabama* and the *Kearsarge*," *Battles and Leaders of the Civil War*, 4 vols. New York: Century, 1884, 1887, 1888.

_____. "The Kearsarge and the Alabama: A New Story of an Old Fight," *The Overland Monthly*, XIV (1875).

Bulloch, James D. *The Secret Service of the Confederate States in Europe; How the Confederate Cruisers were Equipped.* 2 vols. New York: G. P. Putnam's Sons, 1884.

Edge, Frederick Milnes. *An Englishman's View of the Battle Between the Alabama and the Kearsarge: An Account of the Naval Engagement in the British Channel, on Sunday June 19, 1864.* New York: A.D.F. Randolph, 1864.

[Fullam, George Townley.] *The Cruise of the Alabama, Raphael Semmes, Commander, from Her Departure from Liverpool,* July 29, 1862. London, 1864.

Hamersly, Thomas H. S. *Complete Army and Navy Register of the United States of America from 1776 to 1887.* New York: Hamersly, 1888.

Hobson, Henry S. *The Famous Cruise of the Kearsarge: An Authentic Account in Verse of the Battle with the Alabama off Cherbourg, France, on Sunday, June 19, 1864.* Bonds Village, Mass., 1894.

Kell, John McIntosh. "A Yarn from Uncle Bob's Log; or A True Tale of the Alabama," *Burke's Weekly for Boys and Girls.*

————. "Cruise and Combats of the 'Alabama,'" *Battles and leaders of the Civil War,* vol. IV. 4 vols. New York: Century, 1884, 1887, 1888.

————. *Recollections of a Naval Life; Including the Cruises of the Confederate Steamers Sumter and Alabama.* Washington: Neale, 1900.

[Latham, John.] *Narrative of the Cruise of the Alabama, and List of Her Officers and Men, By One of the Crew.* London, 1864.

Miller, Francis T. *The Navies.* ("Photographic History of the Civil War," vol. VI.) New York: Review of Reviews, 1911.

Naval History Division, Navy Dept. Office of the Chief of Naval Operations. *Dictionary of American Naval Fighting Ships.* 2 vols. Washington: U. S. Government Printing Office, 1959, 1963.

Nesser, Robert Wilden. *Statistical and Chronological History of the United States Navy, 1775–1907.* 2 vols. New York: Macmillan, 1909.

Official Records of the Union and Confederate Navies in the War of the Rebellion. Series I, 27 vols.; Series II, 3 vols.; General Index, 1927. Washington: Government Printing Office, 1894–1922.

Parker, William H. *Recollections of a Naval Officer, 1841–1865.* New York: Charles Scribner's Sons, 1883.

[Penhoat, Adm.] "Kearsarge and Alabama: French Official Report, 1864," *The American Historical Review,* XXIII, i (Oct., 1917).

Phelps, Thomas S. "Reminiscences of the Old Navy," *The United Service; A Monthly Review of Military and Naval Affairs,* VII (1882).

Porter, David D. *The Naval History of the Civil War.* New York: Sherman, 1886.

Register of Officers of the Confederate States Navy, 1861–1865. Washington: United States Government Printing Office, 1931.

Roe, Francis Asbury. *Naval Duties and Dsicipline, with the Policy and Principles of Naval Organization.* New York: Van Nostrand, 1865.

Semmes, Raphael. *Service Afloat and Ashore During the Mexican War.* Cincinnati: Wm. H. Moore, 1851.

_____. *Service Afloat; The Remarkable Career of the Confederate Cruisers Sumter and Alabama, During the War Between the States.* New York: P. J. Kennedy, 1900.

Sinclair, Arthur. *Two Years on the Alabama.* Boston: Lee and Shepard, 1896.

Vandiver, Frank E., ed. *Confederate Blockade Running Through Bermuda 1861–1865; Letters and Cargo Manifests.* Austin: The University of Texas Press, 1947.

Newspapers

Atlanta Constitution

Boston Evening Transcript

Boston Journal

The Daily Picayune (New Orleans)

Griffin News

Harper's Weekly; A Journal of Civilization

The Illustrated London News

London Times

Macon Daily Telegraph

Macon Telegraph and Messenger

New York Herald

New York Sun

New York World

Philadelphia Weekly Times

The Spectator (London)

Washington Post

Index

Highlights &
Sidelights
of the
CIVIL WAR

Philip Dorf

Highlights & Sidelights of The Civil War is designed primarily to accent the drama, faith, sacrifice, humor, and heartbreak of The Civil War Period.

Without facts history may become an old wife's tale; yet facts alone are not enough. The story of America's Civil War should stir interest, not smother it and should pulsate with spirit, not statistics.

Facts need not, however, rule out the emotions. There is a proper place in The Civil War Story for the incidents, anecdotes, and digressions which add color and flavor to the record.

An anecdote, a couplet from a 19th century poem or song, a slogan, catchword, or epigram, a memorable phrase from a speech or an editorial — all these are vital threads in the intricate tapestry of Civil War history.

They reveal the manners and morals of the age; they reconstruct its tempo and mood. They mirror the ambitions, follies, and hopes of Abraham Lincoln's and Jefferson Davis's generation. They provide the accompaniment to the chronicle of its failures and, more important, its achievements.

A people's traditions constitute the bedrock of national existence. And upon this foundation may depend not only its prospect of greatness, but even its hope of survival. More than a century ago, Edward Everett (1794 – 1865), U.S. Senator and Millard Fillmore's Secretary of State, said: "And how is the spirit of a free people to be formed and animated and cheered, but out of the storehouse of its historic recollections?"

Highlights & Sidelights of The Civil War aims to provide one key to this storehouse about a critical period in our history.

ISBN: 0-913337-16-1

Southfarm Press

$9.95

P.O. Box 1296, Middletown, CT 06457